What People Are Sa
The 7 Best Things (Happy)

D0200392

"Think of your marriage as a gift-wrapped package that's just arrived in the mail. You rush to open it up and there it is, all laid out in front of you. But then you realize there's something missing: no instructions. This book contains all the instructions you'll ever need. There's wisdom on every page. I especially enjoyed chapter 8, The Rocks."

William Glasser, M.D.
author, *Choice Theory*
president, The William Glasser Institute,
Chatsworth, California

"Family therapists Friel *(The 7 Worst Things (Good) Parents Do)* give tips for a healthy relationship. With their usual wit and incisiveness (and plenty of real-life examples from their years of clinical practice), the authors explain key psychological principles that underpin successful partnerships and also probe the unscientific element of 'magic' that happy couples report. They describe how to avoid common pitfalls and nudge readers toward a better understanding about how early experiences influence romantic relationships. This is a useful resource for anyone in a relationship—be it a healthy or an unhealthy one."

Publishers Weekly

"Buy this book. After reading it, my wife and I had the best dialogue in our thirty-five years of marriage. The Friels show how it is only a matter of degree between awesome and awful relationships."

Jon Carlson, Psy.D., Ed.D.
Distinguished Professor, Governors State University
author, *Time for a Better Marriage* and *Living Love*

"Superb! The Friels have captured the magic of marriage in the context of day-to-day experience. Built on a foundation of sharing and mutual respect, the book utilizes stories to draw a visual image of truly happy couples. An extremely valuable, practical and much needed resource for couples and relationship therapists!"

Dr. Stan Huff
Professor of Counseling, Bradley University, Peoria, Illinois
twenty-year AAMFT clinical member and approved supervisor

"It feels like the Friels have been listening in to our conversations for years! After nearly forty years of marriage, the most joy is in healing those old wounds, not ripping them open. The Friels continue to remind us about how complex good relationships truly are—and how rewarding a marriage can be!"

Nancy McIntyre
San Clemente, California

"Finally! A book that goes right to the core of a couple's intimacy. This is a remarkable book—complex, straightforward, fascinating and clear. I highly recommend it!"

Lawrence Weiss, Ph.D.
director, Sanford Center for Aging, University of Nevada, Reno

"This book is a must for couples who want to move from an 'average' relationship into true relationship depth and happiness. The Friels have a gift for bringing to the forefront the important issues that keep us stuck. Knowing there is something missing, and how to change and grow with it are what this book is about. Thanks Friels— keep on writing!"

Peter Charad
Stenhousemuir, Scotland

"The authors illustrate healthy relationships by sharing with their readers their own poetic love story and stories from their private practice. This book can serve as a springboard into major changes in how we approach our primary relationships. It can also serve as a gentle reminder of our best efforts or aspirations."

Cynthia Stange
Shoreview, Minnesota

"A wonderful resource for couples. The Friels have pinpointed eight of the most crucial issues that go into making up a truly great relationship. Their practical suggestions, based on personal experience, research and clinical experience, are excellent. I highly recommend it."

Pat Love, Ed.D.
author, *The Truth About Love: The Highs, the Lows and How You Can Make It Last Forever*

Some Surprising Things This Book Will Teach You About Relationships . . .

- Disappointment is a good thing for couples.
- There is no such thing as "common sense."
- *Feeling* like hurting your partner is normal. *Doing* it is not okay.
- Dating is a process of hurting and being hurt.
- Having a lot of similar interests is not especially important in a really happy relationship.
- Conflict is a good thing.
- It is not possible to be deeply intimate if your goal is to always be "nice."
- Conflict—especially sexual conflict—is good. It helps people grow.
- We always pair up with emotional equals—you are *not* healthier than your partner.
- A relationship can only be as deep as the shallower of the two of you is able to go.
- One hundred eighty degrees from sick is still sick.
- You can't be married if you're not old enough to date.
- Sexual passion does *not* leave a great relationship after seven years.
- If you aren't willing to divorce your partner, you probably won't have a truly happy relationship with him or her.
- The parent you "like" best may be your biggest problem.
- Many people in affairs need to become more like their spouse rather than having an affair.
- The first child is more like the father, the second child like the mother, and the third child like the marital relationship.
- The ability to be in awe of creation is absolutely essential in having a great relationship.
- If you do everything for everyone else, but never take care of your own needs, no grown-up will want to be in a romantic relationship with you.
- Fear, hurt, shame and loneliness are at the root of marital violence, but they are also at the root of marital bliss.
- If you keep asking *how your partner* can change to make the relationship better, forget it. Nothing will ever get better.

7 THE BEST THINGS (Happy) COUPLES DO

John C. Friel, Ph.D.
Linda D. Friel, M.A.

Health Communications, Inc.
Deerfield Beach, Florida

www.hci-online.com

Library of Congress Cataloging-in-Publication Data

Friel, John C., date.

The 7 best things (happy) couples do / John C. Friel, Linda D. Friel.

p.   cm.

Includes bibliographical references and index.

ISBN 1-55874-953-5 (tp)

1. Marriage. 2. Couples. 3. Love. 4. Man-woman relationships.
I. Title: Seven best things (happy) couples do. II. Friel, Linda D.
III. Title.

HQ734 .F768 2002

306.7—dc21

2001051764

©2002 John C. Friel and Linda D. Friel

ISBN 1-55874-953-5

Publisher: Health Communications, Inc.

3201 S.W. 15th Street

Deerfield Beach, FL 33442-8190

R-04-02

Cover design by Lisa Camp

Inside book design by Dawn Grove

To Love

Other Books by the Authors

The 7 Worst Things (Good) Parents Do

The 7 Best Things (Smart) Teens Do

Adult Children: The Secrets of Dysfunctional Families

An Adult Child's Guide to What's "Normal"

The Grown-Up Man: Heroes, Healing, Honor,
Hurt, Hope

Rescuing Your Spirit: When Third-Grade Morality
Isn't Enough for Christians

The Soul of Adulthood: Opening the Doors

CONTENTS

PREFACE

This book is about both the *magic* and the *science* of relationships. Over the years, we have grown to appreciate the wisdom that both of these contribute to developing healthy relationships. Those who try to do it all by magic often end up dissatisfied, and those who try to do it all by science end up dissatisfied, too. In this book, we will include both, as we might in helping someone through their relationship struggles. Science without magic can be cold and impersonal, and magic without science can be chaotic and confusing.

We have learned over the years the value of stories and fables in helping people get past the defenses that they installed decades ago to protect themselves from whatever shortages they experienced while growing up. We have learned this directly from our mentors, as well as indirectly through the writings of masters such as Milton H. Erickson and Jay Haley. We have tried to sprinkle throughout this book a sufficient number of actual case examples, as well as fables, to not only create some magic in the book, but also to help you understand and integrate what we are trying to get across.

Ten years ago, an audience of professionals in London, England, suggested that we write a book on relationships after hearing us give a workshop on the topic. We had enough material to do a book back then, but we had other projects on the front burner. And although we actually started writing this book in 1997, it got sidetracked yet again. In writing this book, we've come to appreciate the value of these delays, and just how important the last ten years have been for developing and shaping this book. Maybe things do happen just the way they are meant to happen. Nonetheless, it has been a joy to finally get back to it and complete it.

While attending the Milton Erickson Institute's "Evolution of Psychotherapy Conference" in Anaheim, California, in May 2000, we had the pleasure of listening to and learning from some of the most distinguished names in the fields of both individual and family therapy, including Salvador Minuchin, James Masterson, John Gottman, Jay Haley, Chloe Madanes and Thomas Szasz. John Gottman, as many readers know, is the psychologist at the University of Washington who has done some of the most thorough and groundbreaking work on marriage in the past quarter-century. Salvador Minuchin is one of the founding fathers—or grandfathers—of the "systems" approach to family therapy. James Masterson is one of the world's leading experts on working with borderline and narcissistic personality disorders. Jay Haley and Chloe Madanes are also great pioneers in the systems and (Milton) Ericksonian approaches to psychotherapy. And some of you may know of Thomas Szasz, the brilliant psychiatrist who wrote the groundbreaking 1961 article entitled "The Myth of Mental Illness." All of us who work with individuals and families owe a huge debt of gratitude to these giants in the field.

As therapists reading this already know, each couple that comes in for therapy is unique, and no matter how many couples you've seen, it will never cease to be a challenge to try

to help two people strengthen their relationship. We were
both strengthened and enchanted at the above conference
when, in his wise, warm and immensely charming way, still
carrying his Argentinean accent after all these years, distinguished clinician Salvador Minuchin said:

> *And so you see, all marriages are mistakes, that then we
> spend time repairing; and some of us are more successful in
> repairing than others.*

We found this such a warm, compassionate, powerful thing
to say, especially from a man of such stature. So many of us are
seeking the perfect relationship when the perfect relationship
is right in front of us. If only there was a way to get this across
in a book that people could use before and during their relationships rather than *after* the fact.

That is why we wrote this book—to provide some of the
science and magic that we now know go into making a truly
great relationship. In a nation where the divorce rate still hov-
ers around 50 percent as this book goes into print, and where
many couples haven't been away, by themselves, overnight,
without kids or without work, for years, we thought it would
be helpful for couples to read what we have discovered to be
seven (actually eight) of the very best things truly happy
couples do. We hope you enjoy this book, and that your relationships profit from it.

Seven—Plus One

The human brain can "hold onto" approximately seven
things at a time. As we explain in Appendix B, this applies
only to seven unidimensional things, such as circles of different sizes or varying shades of gray. This number is approxi-
mate because the average person can hold onto somewhere

between five and nine things, depending on the capacity of her short-term memory. Seven is a number of biblical proportions for many reasons, but certainly one of them is that our brains are wired for it.

When it comes to lists in self-help books, seven is "a good round number" because, as soon as you get ten or twelve or fifteen things to focus on, you lose your focus! As we picked up this project after putting it aside a few years ago, we decided to go with the "seven" theme of our last two books. When we realized that we actually had eight things that we wanted to emphasize, we decided to go ahead and keep the extra one rather than paring it down, knowing that eight was within the range of the "magic number seven, plus or minus two."

The things that we ultimately decided to look at in more depth are the ones that we have observed to be the most significant ones that couples must address and embrace if they are to become the truly happy couples that they'd like to be. There are certainly others, and certainly other authors or clinicians might emphasize other things. When people come to us for help, these are what we help them look at as they move boldly toward improving their relationships.

And so here they are—the best things truly happy couples do:

1. Be Old Enough to Date
2. Be Sexual
3. Be Willing to Divorce
4. Know How You Chose Each Other
5. Let Yourself Be Astonished
6. Manage Your Fear, Hurt, Shame and Loneliness
7. Own Your Own Part
Plus . . . Let Disappointment Enrich You

This book is divided into five parts. In part I, we paint pictures of how a truly happy relationship looks and feels, and how an unhappy one looks and feels. We have used lists like these in some of our previous work, and have found them to be very effective in helping people troubleshoot their relationships, as well as get an intuitive sense of what they're trying to achieve. In part II, we discuss the stages of love relationships, from dating all the way through to mutuality, as well as the most crucial "rules of the game" of romantic relationships. Taken together, these two sections are some of the most important information that we share with couples who are doing marriage and couple therapy with us.

In part III, we share with you a therapeutic fable that we hope will clear up for many readers the core dilemma we see in therapy, which is the answer to the question: How can I move on into adulthood and have a good life even when my childhood was very painful? This is an essential piece of *couples therapy,* because people who can't move beyond their childhood hurts and wounds will have a difficult time making a mature romantic relationship work.

In part IV, we present and discuss in detail the eight things that we believe go into a truly happy relationship; and in part V, we take one final moment to reinforce for the reader the importance of getting to know and becoming comfortable with your own story, your partner's story, and how those two stories converge.

♥ ♥ ♥

Before you begin, we would like to state a couple of conventions used in this book. We tried to alternate between "him" and "her" or "he" and "she" as best we could, but we didn't keep track. If there is a gender imbalance in the examples and case studies we use, it is not intentional.

When we use the word "marriage" we are referring to *any*

long-term romantic-type relationship. The concepts and examples apply as well to gay couples as they do to straight ones, and any couple in between. We say this despite the fact that people who live together for many years and then eventually get married often discover that their relationship changes dramatically the day after the wedding ceremony. There is something profound about bringing a relationship into an established social structure.

The religions that we were both raised in happened to be Christian, and so our experience is more with Christian ideas and practices as well as "dysfunctions." Most of what we write about applies regardless of what your religious training was or is.

A few brief sections of this book were adapted from a few of our previous books because they were essential in developing the points that we wanted to get across, and they had already been explained to our satisfaction in those previous works. Appendix A is adapted from our detailed explanation of Erik Erikson's developmental stages in our first book, *Adult Children: The Secrets of Dysfunctional Families.* Having a working understanding of these stages—how they really work and what helps us through them—is crucial in understanding the central themes of this book, and so we encourage you to read this appendix, even if you have read it in our other book before. Some of the material on sexuality and spirituality is adapted from *Rescuing Your Spirit: When Third-Grade Morality Isn't Enough for Christians,* and some of the material on accountability, disappointment, and resistance is adapted from *The Soul of Adulthood: Opening the Doors,* while the section on "extremes" is from our book on teens, and the section on "small changes" is from our parenting book.

ACKNOWLEDGMENTS

To all the people with whom we have worked over the years, for sharing your life struggles with us, we give you our sincerest and most respectful thanks. It is surely an honor to have been invited into the details of your relationships, and therefore into your very hearts and souls.

To those who raised us, lived with us as we were growing up, befriended us, and who taught us along the way, we thank you for the gifts of knowledge and relationship. There is no way we could have become who we are without you. As always, we want to give special recognition to James Maddock, Ph.D., University of Minnesota professor and clinical psychologist in private practice, for providing the wisdom and guidance over the years that have allowed us to continue to grow as psychologists, but even more importantly, as human beings, over the past twenty years. It is always hard for us to find the words to describe what an honor it is to know you.

To our children, we thank you for coming into our lives and enriching us simply by your existence. The three of you and your spouses and loved ones are remarkable. There is nothing quite as exciting nor quite as humbling as to be allowed to provide some of the guardianship for another human being as he or she grows into a whole, separate adult. And now that we are a little older, and as time marches on, we say to our grandchildren, "Welcome to this life!"

We want to thank Mary Pietrini, our colleague and friend for so many years, for her encouragement and appreciation of, and occasional critical editing of, our various manuscripts. Thanks also to Peter Charad for his friendship and his support of our work for so many years, and to our dear friend Dearbhla Molloy, whose starring performance as Hannah in Tom Stoppard's *Arcadia* in London inspired us to delight in the mysteries of life, and whose heartrending role as Alice in the premiere of Brian Friel's *Aristocrats* at the Abbey Theater in Dublin, Ireland, in 1979, contributed to the depth of our understanding of forgiveness and grace.

Last, we want to thank Peter Vegso, president of Health Communications, Inc., for being with us for the past seventeen years, and to include Gary Seidler, recently retired from his role as co-owner of HCI, in those same thanks. We thank Lisa Drucker for her competent and wise editorial stewardship of this project; Susan Tobias for her cheerful guiding of us toward agreement on a cover for this book; Erica Orloff for her outstanding editing of the manuscript; Kim Weiss for guiding the promotion of our work; Maria Dinoia for being such a good friend, and for her tireless support of our work in the marketplace; and the art, sales and marketing departments at HCI, for their ongoing efforts. Without all of you, there would be no books.

There are always and only two trains running.
There is life and there is death.
Each of us rides them both.
To live life with dignity,
to celebrate and accept responsibility
for your presence in the world
is all that can be asked of anyone.

AUGUST WILSON
TWO TRAINS RUNNING

Part I

A Portrait of Love

*How do I love thee? Let me
count the ways.
I love thee to the depth and
breadth and height
My soul can reach.*

Elizabeth Barrett Browning
Sonnets from the Portuguese

1

The Explanation

> . . . There is a feeling now, that was not here before,
> and is not just on the surface of things,
> but penetrates all the way through:
> We've won it. It's going to get better now.
> You can sort of tell these things.
>
> —Robert Pirsig
> *Zen and the Art of Motorcycle Maintenance*

After twenty-one years of living together in a marriage, decades of scientific theories and data about relationships, and an amalgam of what we've gathered from our years of working with people in therapy settings, no matter how we think of them or try to write about them, making sense of love relationships can be baffling at times. Is the science flawed? Have we been deluding ourselves all of these years? Or is it simply that the array of successful human

3

possibilities is defined by an infinite number of conceivable genetic combinations? There are over 6 billion people in the world right now, and you'd have to multiply that by another billion to get an estimate of how many types of successful relationships there could be at any given moment in time.

And so, rather than being exhaustive or definitive, this book consists of some of our thoughts about relationships and some of the research on them. Before we send this manuscript to our publisher, scores more will be sent to other publishers to be in print next year, too. This book is just *one* way of putting together some of the things we see. When two people come to us for therapy, they are coming to see what *they* can see, using *us* as catalysts. When they go to someone else, they are going for different catalysts. In the same way, our children are a product of our lives, not yours. Your children are a product of yours, not ours. As obvious as that may seem, we say it because it underscores the crucial part of relationship therapy—that only *you* can improve your intimate relationship. Nobody else can do it for you.

The Patterns of Life

Part of the science of relationships is captured in the principle of *reenactment.* We have a friend who enthusiastically participates in Civil War reenactments, during which he and his compatriots dress up in authentic uniforms from the mid-1800s, brandish authentic Civil War–era weapons, eat the kinds of food that soldiers ate back then and fight the famous battles of the war, to the delight of thousands of onlookers. In the study of relationships, reenactment refers to the fact that the patterns we display as adults are based on patterns that began when we were children. It also helps explain how patterns are passed on from one generation to the next, not only by genetics, but also by *learning*.

On paper, at least, it's fairly simple to comprehend. As a child, you loved to read. At thirty-five years of age, you love to read. As a child, you were active and dominant, and at forty you are still active and dominant. When you were angry as a child, no one listened to you, or they told you to be quiet and go to your room—that a good child does not get angry. At thirty-five years of age, your husband brings you in for marriage counseling because he can't stand your pouting and silences anymore. It explains why, despite making a strong childhood vow to the contrary, a woman who had a controlling father is quite likely to either be very controlling herself, or to marry a controlling man.

As adults mature and deepen across the life span, we are blessed with a gift that replaces and far exceeds the value of the physical prowess that we gradually lose—we gain *wisdom*. In the arena of human affairs, a fair piece of this wisdom comes from understanding, accepting and becoming at peace with our psychological histories. It is common to have either an idealized or a "demonized" picture of our childhoods when we enter our twenties, and to assume that whatever was, was, and that we just have to press on in life. It is normal to begin tripping over the ghosts of our past somewhere between our mid-twenties and our mid-forties. And if we embrace the challenge of deepening and growing, we eventually gain a piercingly clear appreciation of the simultaneous complexity and simplicity of life.

Contrary to what some believe, the goal of growing up, whether or not you had a painful childhood, is *not* to rewrite your psychological history. Not only is it impossible to do so, but it wouldn't be emotionally or spiritually wise even if you could. An interviewer once asked us, "We eventually stop picking partners who fit those painful childhood patterns in any way, shape or form, right?" Our reply was an emphatic "No." The goal isn't to eradicate our childhoods. The goal is to *master* them. If you had a physically abusive, rageful father, your pattern may be to enter relationships with men who then become physically rageful. It doesn't mean you'll always have to marry physically abusive men. Once you've mastered your childhood and live in Emotional Adulthood, you will have the power of *choice* to stay or to leave and move on. But the man you eventually find happiness with may still be more on the stronger/controlling side, but within the healthier range. And, being in Emotional Adulthood, you will have a strong enough core self to maintain your power in the relationship.

The process of "emotionally growing up beyond childhood" and mastering our psychological history is represented in chapter 8, The Rocks. It is a snapshot of the long, rewarding process of growing up and mastering and integrating our history rather than trying to erase it. It is part of the magic of being human. It is man and woman at their best. The two chapters following the one you are now reading are comprised of descriptive lists of what really great love does and does not feel like. These two lists are also designed to tap into the "magic" much more than the "science" of relationships. They are verbal paintings or impressions.

About List I and List II

As you read the two lists that follow in the next two chapters, we urge you to read them more than once. Savor them. Let them soak into your unconscious mind. If you do, perhaps you won't need to read the rest of this book, because painted in these two lists are pictures of what is and what is not part of really great relationships. Reading through the lists, you may notice that there is only one statement that is exactly the same in both lists. The letters and words in the two sentences are identical, and they are in identical order, yet the differences underlying the two represent the cutting edge—*the subtle six- to seven-degree difference*—between a really painful relationship and a really great one.

As you finish with the lists, we suggest that you let yourself pause and reflect on the stirrings in your heart and soul, and spend some time leafing through the pages of your life to see from whence those passions came. When you've done this, tell your partner about that part of you. Share it with your partner. Thus intimacy begins.

It is through connecting one heart to another, around seemingly small things, that love grows.

2

List I:
What Really Great Love Looks Like

". . . You make me sick. I hate your guts."
I used every cuss word I could think of
for him and his guy. Then I hung up.
I don't remember him saying anything.

I didn't blame her. Change the details
and she said about the same thing
I would have said if we had lost.

—Mary Matalin and James Carville
All's Fair: Love, War and Running for President

I Know That I Am in Love with You Because/Because of/When . . .

1. I used to get so mad at you because you left the tops off of everything. Now, when I reach for the juice and the cover falls off, I smile and think, "Oh. She's been here recently. She's in my life. I'm so glad."

2. I look at you after twenty years and wonder how it works that it can still be as exciting as the day we met.

3. When I'm in San Francisco on business, and I see a young couple in love, entranced with the magic, all I think of is you.

4. You fight with me, you hate me at times, and then you stop and smile because you remembered how I made you laugh when you were so scared about that job interview.

5. You are as sexy to me as the day we met, even when we're both too tired to make love.

6. You tell me when I'm being foolish.

7. You like Kevin Spacey.

8. You are comforted that Jimmy Carter and Gerald Ford are still here.

9. You would never take dancing lessons on your own, but you love the ones we took together.

10. You think computers and wires and buttons are ridiculous, and you secretly like me because I know how to make them work.

11. When you and the other guys tease about makeup and hormones, you can laugh but still leave them with the

subtle impression that to you, these are as important as oil changes and football, because they are important to me.

12. You are sexy because you don't try to be.
13. You don't whine when you're in pain.
14. You can watch me cry at the end of the movie, and you act like you didn't notice, but I know you did.
15. You trudge off to work in the dead of winter when it's twenty degrees below zero, and I'm worrying about your sensitivity to the cold, and then my anxiety disappears as I get ready for work in a bathroom infused with the intoxicating hint of an adult woman's perfume.
16. You enter a room full of people and start the conversation going, making our presence accepted, and include me just when I feared I might disappear.
17. You cajoled and harped and seduced me into taking that job I thought I couldn't do, and it turned into what I love to do more than anything in the world.
18. You fought me tooth and nail about the value of making our house a home, and you never gave up one inch, until I gave in and realized that it was one of the best things that ever happened to me.
19. You're so female.
20. I hate your smelly running shoes, and love them because they're so male.
21. That crinkle in your eyes when you smile.
22. Your smell.
23. The sound of your breathing in the middle of the night.

24. How excited you were when you ran that race you never thought you'd be able to run.
25. Your spirit soars as we enter the desert.
26. How scared you get about things that don't scare me.
27. You take such good care of us.
28. You love my little dog after you thought you never could.
29. You thought of my son.
30. My daughters cried in your arms.
31. You fell in love with my dream before you ever saw it.
32. You never told me I needed help, but were there as I struggled to find it.
33. You were ready to divorce me.
34. You stood with me at my father's funeral.
35. Your love of the ocean, which terrifies me.
36. Your greatest anxiety comes from your care for me.
37. Your laugh.
38. The way you touch me.
39. You pay the bills and taxes and make the mortgages happen.
40. Your depth is expressed in the care with which you grace our home.
41. Your sense of style.
42. The magic that you write.
43. Your dutiful compassion toward your friends.
44. Your silence.
45. The clutter and chaos that I've learned to tolerate.
46. How your hectic pace and my quiet thoughtfulness can fit together like keystones.
47. You like to ski, and I can't get warm enough in wintertime.

48. You get mad at me when I'm preoccupied, because you want me.
49. You kept your dignity at that social engagement when few could have.
50. The way you still lust for me.
51. The trance you go into when the sun sets below the mountains above the lake.
52. The way you cry whenever a movie or story or radio program hints at your pain with your father.
53. No matter how difficult it has been over so many years, you always drive me crazy with passion.
54. You show me yourself at your weakest.
55. You are so strong.
56. I never went to the movies when I was little, and you take me there all the time.
57. I never had a home, and you made one for me.
58. You are the best friend I have ever had.
59. You hardly ever tell me how you voted.
60. You think I'm cute.
61. You wore those silly-looking pants on our first date, and you still wonder why it makes me smile.
62. You adore every inch of me.
63. We like who we are together.
64. After all these years, I still can't figure out why.

3

List II:
What Really Great Love
Does Not Look Like

All that remained of their original passion
was a faint crackle of electricity animating
their insults, their drab swipes at one another.
That was all that showed anyway.

—Jonathan Lethem
Motherless Brooklyn

This Relationship Feels
So "Off" Because . . .

1. You have been leaving the tops off of everything for
   ten years and I resent you more now than ever. When

15

I reach for the juice and the cover falls off, I burn inside and wonder how you can keep betraying me after I've told you OVER AND OVER to stop it, and you never do.

2. I look at you after twenty years and wonder how I can take another five.

3. When I'm in San Francisco on business, and I see a young couple in love, entranced with the magic, I envy them and think of how great it would be to have a torrid affair just for the heck of it.

4. You fight with me, you hate me at times, and then you tell me that you can't think of one good reason that we're still together.

5. We hardly ever have sex, and when we do, it's just that—having sex. I'm secretly relieved that we're both too tired most of the time.

6. You tell me when I'm being foolish all the time. That's all I ever hear from you.

7. You like Kevin Spacey, who I think is highly overrated.

8. You are comforted that Jimmy Carter and Gerald Ford are still here, and I couldn't care less. I'd rather be fishing.

9. You would never take dancing lessons on your own, and when I finally nagged you into doing it, you sabotaged it the entire time and didn't really try. I felt let down and embarrassed.

10. You think computers and wires and buttons are ridiculous. You tell all of your friends what a "little boy" I am.

11. When you and the other guys tease about makeup and hormones, you say you're "just kidding," but your nonverbal messages clearly say "contempt."

12. You aren't sexy because you try too hard to be.

13. You're such a baby when you're in pain.

14. You peer into my eyes like a prying, intrusive mother to see if I cried during the movie, but I didn't, and I certainly wouldn't dare do it in front of someone who has made me her "emotional project."

15. You trudge off to work in the dead of winter when it's twenty degrees below zero, and as I get ready for work, all I can think is, "I wish she'd change that perfume— I've hated it for fifteen years but have never told her."

16. You enter a room full of people and start the conversation going, making *your* presence known, as usual. Why do I still bother to go places with you? You're so obnoxious!

17. You cajoled and harped and seduced me into taking that job when I knew I couldn't do it. I discovered I *could* do it. But don't think you have anything to do with my success.

18. You fought me tooth and nail about the value of making our house a home, and you never gave up one inch. Yeah, it all looks nice. But did we really *need* it?

19. You're so female that I can't stand it. Don't you get it?

20. I hate your smelly running shoes, and you have NEVER done anything about them.

21. That crinkle in your eyes when you smile makes you look too "cutesy."

22. Your smell has always bothered me.

23. Can't you *do* something about the sound of your breathing in the middle of the night?

24. You were so excited when you ran that race you never thought you'd be able to run. So, will you *ever* stop acting so childish?

25. Every time we drive into the desert, you say it makes your spirit soar, and I catch myself saying, silently, "Okay! Okay! Let's just drive on without making such a big spiritual deal out of everything!"

26. You're afraid of everything. Get a grip.

27. You say you're trying to take good care of us, but I wish you'd just take care of yourself for a while.

28. The fact that you can't find any warmth in your heart for my little dog isn't really the issue. It's that you don't seem to have any warmth in your heart for me at all anymore.

29. You never think of my son.

30. My daughters don't like you.

31. You told me my dream was impractical.

32. You nag me to death about my drinking. Why don't you get some help for your "nagging addiction"?

33. You're too dependent to ever divorce me.

34. You went to my father's funeral and made calls on your cell phone the whole time.

35. You're obsessed with the ocean.

36. Stop worrying about me. You're neurotic.

37. Your laugh needs improvement.

38. The way you touch me makes me angry.

39. Yes, you pay the bills and taxes and make the mortgages happen, but that's what you're *supposed* to do.

40. For the life of me, I can't figure out why you keep talking about the importance of "creating a home." Creating a home? What about politics and other important things?

41. Your sense of style just doesn't do it for me.

42. The stuff that you write needs major work.

43. You spend too much energy helping your friends. What about me?

44. Your silence is a sign of an emotional problem.

45. The clutter and chaos that you create is keeping you from being the successful person I thought I was marrying.

46. We're just too different.

47. You like to ski, and I can't get warm enough in wintertime. What does *that* tell you about us?

48. You get mad at me when I'm preoccupied. Hell, I'm trying to save us from your latest folly!

49. When she was so obnoxious at the party, you should have told that woman off! When will you ever learn?

50. The way you lust for me is a turn-off.

51. Watching that sunset every day? Does it always have to stop my life?

52. Okay. You and your father didn't quite connect. I get it. I get it!

53. It has been so difficult over so many years, that I just don't feel anything for you anymore.

54. You show me yourself at your weakest. Why do you do that? I want someone who is solid.

55. You think you are so strong.

56. You take me to the movies all the time. I never went to the movies when I was little. All of the other kids went. My parents thought movies were a waste of time. I learned not to be frivolous. I don't want to see movies.

57. I never had a home, and I still don't feel like I have one.

58. I hear people talk about their spouse as their best friend. I think they're deluding themselves.

59. You wouldn't be dumb enough to vote for *that* candidate, would you?

60. It doesn't seem like you're attracted to me.

61. You wore those silly-looking pants on our first date, and you still don't get it.

62. I want to be adored by someone.

63. We look good in public.

64. After all these years, I still can't figure out why.

Part II

There Is an Interesting Story Behind Everything

When we have found all the mysteries and lost all the meaning, we will be alone, on an empty shore.

Tom Stoppard
Arcadia

4

The Man, the Woman and the Sea

But it is not really our genes that are failing us.
It is our heart that is failing us. The central value
of Western romantic chivalry was *courtesy*—a
refinement of feeling which is capable of
leading romantic love to the threshold
of divine love and mystic union.

—Charles Upton
Hammering Hot Iron: A Spiritual Critique of Bly's Iron John

In *The Soul of Adulthood,* we wrote of the simple, extraordinary magic that comes to couples from their unconscious minds when they are in tune with themselves and each other in this true story about a couple we know. This man and woman had been together for several years and were creating a deep and abiding love for one another. They had shared many a struggle and many a joy. As they got to know each other, the man told her how much fun he and his brother and sister had swimming in the ocean every summer, and how important water had become to him during his childhood. The woman shared with him her fear of water, and of how her father had not been a very good swimming teacher because of his impatience and gruffness. But swimming outdoors in cold clear lakes and thundering ocean surf had become so deeply embedded in the man's soul that he was secretly disappointed that the woman wasn't as excited as he was about it.

They discussed these things for several years but always came to the same frustrating conclusion. The woman did not like being in the water and felt misunderstood and angry. The man, on the other hand, felt betrayed deep inside by her reluctance. But he kept trying to get her to change because he was convinced that their relationship would be ruined if she was never able to join him in the ocean as his brother and sister had.

One day when they were at the beach on a fairly calm day, the man tried every trick he could think of to talk the woman into going into the ocean with him. Purely as a gift to him the woman finally agreed, and as they began to walk into the surf together a swell came out of nowhere and washed over them, forcing water into her breathing passages. When he saw the terror in her eyes the man felt awful, and he vowed to himself and to her that he would never pressure her like that again. At the same time, the woman saw the remorse in the man's eyes and heard the

sincerity in his voice, and the shared instant of simultaneous vulnerability swept over them graciously like a wave of
healing light.

The next morning as he was swimming in the surf below
the lanai of their hotel room, he waved to her as she read the
morning newspaper and sipped her coffee, taking in the
gentle breeze, and she smiled and waved back. And then
from nowhere and everywhere inside of him hundreds of
disconnected pieces suddenly gathered and formed an image
of completion. He realized that when he was a child, all of
that time spent in the boiling surf, or in the cool, dark, mys-
tical water underneath the waves, was his way of soothing
the fear and hurt that he frequently felt in his family, and
that the secrets he shared with his brother and sister were
not just about the ocean and its magical healing properties.
As his mind eased back into the here and now, all of those
disconnected fragments of pain and confusion were transformed into a single, deep, focused feeling of peace, for he
realized that the pain of his childhood was behind him, and
the beautiful mystery of his relationship with this woman
did not demand retreat into a watery sanctuary. He no
longer needed someone in the ocean with him to ease his
pain. It was more than enough to swim by himself and to
simply love her.

At that same moment, while she comfortably read her
newspaper and sipped her coffee on their lanai overlooking
the beach, the woman realized that while this man was in
certain ways like her father, he was very different in many
ways, especially in that he was willing and able to see the
fear in her eyes, to acknowledge it, to acknowledge his

mistake, and to put her safety and comfort above his own need to have her swim with him. In that instant, an old wound inside of her healed and her spirit felt light. It felt like magic to both of them. And indeed, it was.

5

The Magic and Science
of Relationships

People destined to meet will do so, apparently by
chance, at precisely the right moment.

—Ralph Waldo Emerson

Poets argue that when we try to unravel the mysteries of
a rainbow, we destroy its essence. Scientists argue that if we
don't try, we remain prisoners of the very forces that we so
admire. How can we, as human beings, reconcile our innate
capacity to view creation through the lenses of metaphor
and poetry with our equally inherent ability to analyze,
synthesize, explain, predict and control? Is it even possible
to write a book that is about both the magic and the science
of relationships?

Where is the magic in relationships when we study them

so carefully that we can predict with startling accuracy whether or not a couple will survive the first ten years of marriage? Where is the magic in identifying, naming and painstakingly counting hundreds of facial expressions, types of body postures, intonations and inflections of voice? If we pick apart the rainbow of relatedness, what will be left? Numbers on a computer screen? Beta weights in a multi-variate analysis of thousands of tiny behaviors? Lines on a graph or chart? Is this, after all is said and done, what our relationships are about?

Science and art, magic and numbers—they do go together at some level, because at some level, they are simply ways to describe the same phenomenon. And therein lies the magic. Like William Shakespeare and Abraham Lincoln, Albert Einstein was a magician, but he was able to apply numbers to it, and so we called it science. The universe is magic, and it is, in our puniness, our job to unravel it. The more we understand it, the more magic is revealed to our amazement and delight—which is all a good relationship is about. Psychologist John Gottman can predict with 94 percent accuracy whether a relationship will "make it" or not, based on, among other things, the ratio of positive to negative interactions between partners over the long haul.[1] And yet this fact does not diminish the lovers' magic one iota, because for each of us, finding and maintaining such a relationship is experienced as magic, whether numbers are applied to it or not—just like Einstein's universe.

As many of us are already well aware, undisciplined talent usually results in either nothing, or in chaos. You may be born with a marvelous musical talent, but if you never learn the skills and discipline required to write music or to play an instrument, you will never make the marvelous music that is locked up in your chromosomes. If you, like all human beings, have an innate desire for healthy, deep, loving relationships, but are never taught by example how to have them, then science tells us that you will have a difficult time having them. It is therefore with much dismay that we hear so many people say, "I don't want to learn about relationships. We just have to *be* together, and it will work out." In the relationship world, these are unfortunate famous last words.

The Science of Psychology Does Have Something to Offer

Some people scoff at what psychology has discovered about human behavior over the last century. And there is certainly some justification for scoffing at what popular "psychobabble" books have preached over the past forty years. But the fact remains that within the fuzzy borders of the field of psychology lie some very important kernels of wisdom. For example, over the preceding decades, in study after study, it has been shown that people who try to live by some of those kernels produce children who do better in school, have more impulse control, are more flexible in their approach to solving problems, are better able to relate to others, and will therefore be happier and more successful when they grow up.

In the past ten years, more and more children have grown

up with impulse control problems, at least in part because they are being raised by parents who are barely around enough to raise them—parents who fall victim to the belief that if their children are enrolled in every possible outside activity known to humanity, they will grow up to be healthy, well-adjusted children. The net result is children who have been abandoned, neglected, overworked and left alone too much. This spells disaster. We were heartened to read a few months ago that parents have actually begun to reverse this dangerous trend.

Not all children and families fall prey to this destructive mind-set. Some parents choose to limit the number of activities in which their children are involved, simply because they recognize it isn't good for their children to be overextended. Why? Because they either grew up in very healthy families where taking care of oneself was valued, or because they read some study or expert opinion that suggested they should try to achieve some balance in their lives, and they took the advice to heart and implemented it despite the difficulties in doing so.

Walter Mischel's Delay of Gratification

When Walter Mischel of Stanford University conducted his groundbreaking research on delay of gratification in children in the 1960s, it fascinated psychologists around the world. Equally fascinating is how Mischel's research is currently being dusted off and widely cited because we are finally recognizing how damaged Americans have become in this arena. A quick summary of Mischel's findings suggests that four-year-olds who can't wait a few minutes for a larger reward, choosing instead a smaller, immediate reward, tend to differ significantly from others *when they are eighteen.*[2]

As teenagers, the kids who couldn't wait were still unable to delay gratification, they did poorly in school, had more attention problems, didn't get along with other kids as well, were more easily frustrated, acted out more and so on. In other words, parents who don't teach young ones how to wait (much of this is learned by observing parents' behavior), and who don't exert leadership and limits with young children, produce teenagers and young adults who are socially, emotionally and oftentimes academically less competent than others.

These scientific findings revealed in Mischel's lab have immediate relevance for anyone connected with children today, years after the research was completed. And as we will demonstrate later in this book, they have relevance for couples, too. The ability to forego gratification and soothe one's discomfort is a key skill required to develop deep adult intimacy.

John Gottman's "Emotional Flooding"

John Gottman's research has shown that once two people are "emotionally flooded," their continued interactions will nearly always be destructive.[3] Emotional flooding occurs when your emotions begin to get out of control, and is accompanied by increased heart rate and blood pressure, heart pounding, rapid breathing and muscle tension, among other symptoms. It is experienced as wanting to run, feeling overwhelmed, feeling like you might do or say something you'll later regret, seeing red, etc. That's one of the most useful pieces of news we've ever heard. It is very useful when we're helping couples learn to manage their conflicts. Imagine the strategy difference. If interactions while flooded are almost always destructive, it would behoove couples to literally "sleep on it" rather than staying up later and later in successively more damaging attempts to "get it resolved" or to "get closure." Interestingly, it requires a certain degree of Mischel's "delay of gratification" in order to pull this off, too. Sometimes people have so much anxiety (fear) that they don't believe they can get through the night until the argument "is finished." When they become convinced that this research may also apply to them, they find it easier to delay gratification, and thus avoid flooding and therefore avoid damaging their relationship.

There Is No Such Thing As Common Sense

It is a universal human tendency to lose sight of what we're doing and where we're going in the heat of battle. This is certainly the case when it comes to the role played by our own childhoods in determining the success of our current relationships.

It is perfectly normal, although quite unfounded, for a person to say the following: "I don't know why I keep getting into one terrible marriage after another. My parents had a wonderful marriage and my childhood was idyllic." We also understand why it is so common to hear a television commentator act dumbfounded at the breaking report of some family or school atrocity. But, for the most part, people from healthy, functional families do not go home after a stressful day and murder each other with axes or shoot their fellow students with automatic weapons. We can only think of two reasons that someone would do such things. Either the person (1) has some kind of physical, organic nervous system damage, caused by either genetics or some environmental trauma, or (2) there are serious shortages in the structure or function of the family system in which the person lives.

In the early 1980s, when we were first married, there was the tragic case of a man who lived in the very upscale St. Paul suburban community of North Oaks, Minnesota. He went home one day and murdered his entire family with a gun and then killed himself. Our understanding is that he had terminal cancer and was distraught at the thought of his not being able to provide adequately for his family. Wracked and blinded by deep despair, the only solution he could see was to kill everyone and then himself.

The bottom line is that it is not the least bit unusual for a man or a woman to become blindly distraught as they are coming to grips with their own premature death. This is normal. It is also a choice point. Everybody is the same up until this point. Now, they separate into *at least* two groups:

1. Those who go home and kill their families and themselves; or

2. Those who go home and talk to their wives or husbands about how scared and desperate they're feeling, how they were so scared and desperate that they even contemplated an atrocity, but that they knew those feelings were just signs of how big the despair is, and how much they needed to talk about it and cry together with the ones they love and trust.

Common sense tells some people that a person who batters an infant is a monster, or worse, possessed. *Science* tells us something very different:

1. That the distance between an infant batterer and a nonbatterer is only a split second;

2. That nonbatterers can admit that they *feel like* battering; and

3. Can differentiate between *feeling like battering* and the much more dangerous *act of battering;* and that

4. They are big enough to *face and manage their shame* and not hide it.

Everyone who has the ability to access their true feelings is aware of having *felt like* they could harm their child. Grownups simply share those feelings, knowing that to share them will divest the feelings of their power to create action. Grownups also have enough maturity and ego strength to ask for help, as in: "I'm at my wits' end. Would you please take the baby for a couple of hours so I can get a break? If I don't get a break, I fear I'll do something I'll regret for the rest of my life."

Systems and Blinders

There are certain ways that *human systems* operate, and they are as scientific and predictable as are the behaviors of bacteria or viruses that invade the body. For example, it is perfectly normal for each of us to have *blinders* that keep us from seeing parts of the system. It isn't terribly disconcerting, then, to hear a man say, "I can't possibly have a problem with my anger. Both of my parents were the most gentle, docile people on Earth."

A blinder results from a complex series of interactions over a long period of time. A child who is treated like a princess by her father is being seduced and subtly exploited by both parents, but who would be aware of that while it was going on? Who at the time could anticipate that years later, this pattern would account for why she can't seem to have a healthy long-term relationship with a man? When she is an adult, who would expect her to be able to connect her current intimacy problems with what felt so good when she was little? After all, everyone wants to feel special. What's so bad about being "the most special of all"?

Salvador Minuchin[4] recounts the story told by José Ortega y Gasset about the time Admiral Robert Peary was mushing towards the North Pole. He took a fix on the stars, followed his compass due north all day long, set up camp and then that night took a fix on the stars again. He had been traveling south! How could this be? Peary later discovered that he had been on a giant ice floe that was drifting south! It is the near-perfect metaphor for how hard it can be at times to see why we're doing what we're doing. A blinder isn't the result of gross stupidity. It is a normal part of being human. The word "denial" has evolved into one of the more pejorative words that can be applied to a person, implying that if we are "in denial," we must have been emotionally damaged beyond repair. Denial is actually a positive mechanism used for a purpose.

If we put blinders back into perspective—as a normal part of our complex psychology and as having a positive function—it gets a lot easier for each of us to look at ourselves without overloading with shame. This, paradoxically, makes it infinitely easier to dismantle blinders when the time is right. We have always had the sincerest respect for each person's symptoms, defenses, blinders and addictions, because these were "installed by the user" for a very good reason.

After all, it would be pretty difficult, even frightening, for a little girl to say:

When my daddy treats me like a princess I feel good and bad inside at the same time. It makes my brother and sister mad at me, and I think Mom has started to compete with me for Daddy's attention. But it feels so good to be special and there are so many rewards for it—I get to go to the club with him and hang out with all of his buddies, and they think I'm the greatest. And Daddy comes to all of my school activities, and the gifts I get are always just a little nicer than anyone else's. I feel guilty about that, but after all, I am special. But I know that isn't fair, and I can see how it hurts my brother's and sister's feelings, and deep down inside, it makes me sad.

Elisabeth Kübler-Ross's[5] stages of coming to terms with dying are so well-known that many people no longer know that she's the one who first identified them. They are:

1. Denial

2. Anger

3. Bargaining

4. Depression

5. Acceptance

Denial is such a crucial part of life because sometimes life is overwhelming. Denial is identical to the breaker switches or fuses in your home's electrical system. When the current reaches dangerous levels, the current is shut off. That's denial. Being told that your life will cease to exist in six months is just such an overload. Discovering that your mother is having an affair, or that your father is sexually abusing your sister, or that your older brother is addicted to cocaine and is in danger of dying from an overdose or in a drug deal gone bad are all pretty good reasons to build a blinder or two.

Part of becoming a strong, clear adult is to de-mythologize our childhoods. This includes gently dismantling the myths we have about Mom and Dad. Children look at the world through the eyes of a child. For example, in my childhood naivete, I may trust all authority figures and believe that they would never hurt me. Or, I might build the opposite myth, that all authority figures are "bad," and that none of them could ever be trusted. As you move into adulthood, these extremes must be replaced with a clearer, more realistic, more accurate belief that *"some* authority figures can be trusted *a lot* of the time, and *some* can *hardly ever* be trusted."

And Back to the Magic

There will always be blinders and denial in how we construct our realities. Sometimes it just doesn't serve us well to be too practical and literal. Sometimes "looking the other way" isn't destructive. Sometimes it's the best thing to do. Consider the thousands of inspirational stories that never would have materialized had the hero of the story not had some denial and stubbornness about his or her personal limitations. "You'll never fly." "You'll never get a book published." "You'll never pass that exam." "You'll never have a really great relationship with a man." "You'll never be able to stop drinking." We'd be millionaires many times over if we had a dollar for every time we heard these.

The magic in life comes from its unpredictability and incomprehensibility—from the fact that every new scientific discovery creates more questions than it answered. There are certain commonalities to really great relationships, but they are pretty broadly described. And just when we believe we have it all pinned down and figured out, we learn something new that changes the whole picture.

6

Hurting and Being Hurt—And Other Crucial Stages of Love

Moreover, from the moment they saw each other
for the first time until he reiterated his
determination a half century later, they never had the
opportunity to be alone or to talk of their love.

—Gabriel Garcia Marquez
Love in the Time of Cholera

Y ou have to kiss a lot of frogs before you find your prince or princess. Not that everyone you date until you meet the love of your life is a frog. But each of us has an unconscious blueprint of an ideal mate, and it truly is unconscious—beyond the comprehension of our conscious mind. In this chapter, we will take you on a journey through four stages that lead from the first date to a deep and satisfying lifetime relationship.

Stage I: Dating—
A Process of Hurting and Being Hurt

A man came to us and asked, "I've been divorced for a year now, and I think I'm ready to get back in and try a little dating. What I'd like to know from you is, how can I avoid the pain of dating? How can I be healthier so that dating isn't so hard?"

Our answer to the first question was, "You can't." You can't avoid the pain of dating, because *dating, by definition, is a process of hurting and being hurt.* The process of finding a mate is a pretty scary proposition for most of us. As we'll see in a later chapter, it isn't really possible to find a long-term mate and have it work out until we have clarified a significant chunk of our identity, which is why the survival rates for very young marriages are so low. Clarifying one's identity is no small task. The hopeful part about the human race is that despite how difficult dating and pairing may be, and despite how much pain we've already endured in past relationships, most of us continue to "forge ahead with great vigor," as JFK often said.

When people come to us for relationship therapy, they often want to know if what they're experiencing is normal. They want us to help them make sense out of what is happening to them. They want their confusion and anxiety to diminish. They want to know why having relationships can be so hard. It's hard because no matter how experienced you are, or how grown up you are, dating is an extremely interesting and complex selection process that requires big emotional risks. This means that the more emotionally resilient you are, the easier the process will be, but it will never be easy.

Ending It

You go out with someone for the first time. You like each other. You go out again. You find things in common. You eventually kiss goodnight. But something is missing. Your heart's just not in it. He's a nice guy, but not the right one for you. This is the moment everyone dreads. After the fourth date, you turn to him as you're driving home and say, "I've really enjoyed getting to know you these past few weeks. You are a very interesting, kind, attractive man. But my heart's just not in it. Rather than keep dating and confuse both of us, I think this will have to be our last date." If we are to have integrity, this is pretty much what we must say, but that doesn't make it any easier. After all, who wants to hurt somebody else's feelings if it can be avoided?

If you struggle a lot with boundaries, if you experienced a lot of emotional abandonment growing up, or if you didn't have good role models for this kind of intimate communication when you were younger, this ending of an early-stage dating relationship will be particularly difficult for you. But consider the alternatives. When someone says, "Let's just be friends," they sometimes mean it. But too often what they mean is, "I'm not romantically attracted to you, but it's too hard for me to end it and let both of us move on, so I'll just gradually drift away and hope you do the same. Then, I won't have to feel like the bad guy." It is perhaps one of the crueler maneuvers that people use in this "end of the relationship" scenario.

Or there is the person who finds so many things about you so annoying that she just can't stand you, but she keeps stringing you along because she doesn't have anything better right now, and she can't stand being alone. So instead, she constantly takes potshots at you, and you can feel her contempt and disgust every time you're near her. What she should say is what the woman in our first example said, but she doesn't have the courage to say it—so instead, you suffer. And your part, of course, is that you stay and put up with it, perhaps for the same reasons. There may be fifty ways to leave your lover, as Paul Simon wrote, but there are only a couple of ways that we'd recommend.

A Selection Process

As another song implies, we need to look at love from both sides—from win and lose. We need to be out there in the world taking risks or we'll never learn what is a good fit for us. The process of dating is a selection process. As we date, we are interviewing each other for what could be a lifelong arrangement. In the beginning, we are *attracted* to each other based on looks and mannerisms—we are physically drawn to each other. We write more about this later. Then, we start to compare *interests* and look for common ground. As that proceeds, we begin to negotiate our individual *needs* as we attempt to build an "us" while keeping the "me" unique. As the relationship deepens, questions of our personal *values* emerge and must be negotiated.

All the while that we are driving to the restaurant, chatting over dinner, enjoying a movie together, discussing politics afterwards, holding hands on the way to the car and giving a kiss goodnight that's "just right" or somehow "just off," we are sending and receiving thousands of bits of information to each other. *He held the door open for me. I like that,* could be one response. Another date might think to herself, *He held the door open for me. Does he think I'm a weak, helpless young thing?* A man thinks, *I can't take my eyes off her smile,* or *Amazing. We voted for the same presidential candidate. There was a fifty-fifty chance of that happening.* One woman thinks, *I wish he'd put his arm around me and pull me a little closer to him. I'm too nervous to make the first move here, but am I ever ready!* Another woman might think, *Thank God he doesn't seem to be one of those "huggy-touchy" types. I like sitting right where I am, for the moment.*

As these thousands of interactions and transactions take place over the coming weeks and months, we will begin to build up an *image* of the relationship, which we then compare to that unconscious image stored deep inside. Each of us looks to see if enough of our needs are being met, and whether or not our partner's needs are being met. We each line up our values and see what kind of a fit we have. As the relationship continues, it will either begin to deepen, or it will remain shallow, stagnate and eventually wither away.

Stage II: We're the Same!

During the honeymoon phase of any relationship, we tend to put on the blinders of love, which is a normal and good thing to do. John Gottman found that couples are in trouble when they can no longer remember many of the good things that attracted them in the beginning, or many of the ecstatic, intoxicating feelings from the early weeks of the relationship.[6] So it is essential for the early bonding process that we see each other through rose-colored glasses—up to a point. You come bounding into your apartment and excitedly tell your roommate that you've just had a date with the most incredible guy, and that the thing that is *so* amazing is that, "We're alike on just about *everything!* He likes David Mamet films; *I* like David Mamet films! He can't stand brussels sprouts; *I* can't stand brussels sprouts! He loves to ski; *I* love to ski! Oh, I could go on for hours and hours. It's almost too amazing to be true. I must be the luckiest woman in the world!"

As we said, it is very important for two people in a romantic relationship to see themselves as the same. But realistically, if the two people were *that* much the same, there wouldn't be much of a relationship. In *Existential Sexuality,* philosopher Peter Koestenbaum wrote:

> . . . *the weak and immature, those who are not ready for love, will collapse under the weight of the independence of their beloved. The independence of the other consciousness permanently assures me that I am not alone in this world.*[7]

In other words, if we were exactly alike, if there were no struggle or conflict between us, if every decision we made was the exact one that our partner would have made, then there will be no dynamic tension in the relationship. And without dynamic tension, there really *is* no relationship. You would simply have two people who are completely fused with one another, losing their separate identities in the process.

Human beings have two competing urges—one is to be separate and unique, the other is to fuse with others and thus never be alone. The dynamic tension between these two seeming opposites provides the endless energy reserves that fuel us from birth to death. By definition, a relationship is a connection between two separate entities, not a fusion of two amoebas who decided that it would be better to be one entity instead of two. At the same time, the ability to "be extremely close while remaining separate" is, paradoxically, what allows deep feelings of connection to occur at moments of heightened intimacy—a moment of increased awareness of self paired with a simultaneous increased awareness of the other.

The value of this second stage of seeing our beloved as nearly identical to ourselves is that it builds connections and creates the glue that can be drawn on later to help keep us together when we encounter rough seas. Couples who tell their story over and over again to each other, warmly and fondly, are much more likely to endure than ones who don't—or worse, who can't. And so we see each other as nearly identical. We like the same foods, like the same sports, have the same political beliefs, like the same kinds of people, enjoy the same art and music and have similar tastes in decorating. Or so it seems. This is an excellent early stage, but by no means the final one.

Stage III: Power Struggles— "Wait a Minute! We're Different!"

The honeymoon is over when you start bumping into your differences. She says, "He *said* he loves skiing, but he never wants to go. I had visions of us skiing every weekend in the winter. But we haven't gone once this season." He says, "She told me that when we moved in together, she wanted us to be equal partners in putting our mark, our identity, into how the place is furnished. When I got home this evening I noticed that my two favorite paintings had been moved to the downstairs guest room, where no one will ever see them. It doesn't feel like I have an equal say in this at all."

Here is a small sampling of some of the most common power struggles that people get into, to one degree or another. See if any of them sound familiar to you.

- How much time we spend together vs. How much time we spend apart
- Being on time vs. Being late
- Your stuff (and everything about it) vs. Your stuff (ditto) (including where it's stored, how much of it you leave out, etc.)
- To hold hands in public vs. To not have public displays of affection
- Being neat and tidy vs. Being messy and disorganized
- Wanting to socialize all the time vs. Wanting a more focused, selective social life

- Expressing emotions comfortably vs. Being more reserved and translating emotions intellectually
- I want to pick the movie vs. *I* want to pick the movie
- You leave the toilet seat up vs. You leave the toilet seat down
- How could you vote for that candidate? vs. How could you vote for *that* candidate?

How often have you heard someone say, "We fight about the stupidest things! I'd be embarrassed to let others in on that part of our relationship." Our response is simply, "Perhaps you aren't a grown-up yet. These *are* the things that grown-ups fight about. Life *is* the little day-to-day details that all add up over the years, so why *wouldn't* you fight about little stuff? That's what *everyone* fights about." Remember what Salvador Minuchin said:

And so you see, all marriages are mistakes, that then we spend time repairing; and some of us are more successful in repairing than others.[8]

Marriage is not really a mistake, it's just that conflict is a necessary and inherent part of any relationship, and couples who are able to resolve their power struggles without destroying each other in the process, or without losing their identity in the process, are the successful "repairers" about whom Minuchin speaks.

This power struggle phase of a relationship goes on for years, but not necessarily with the same intensity. As time passes and relationships mature, many successful couples have "chewed on" and worked through many of their long-standing conflicts. He says, "She's still late two-thirds of the time, but rarely by more than fifteen minutes anymore. I find if I just wait quietly out in the car and greet her cheerfully when she comes out, it lowers her anxiety and mine, and the rest of the day is fine. We've never missed a flight, nor have we missed the beginning of a movie or play. I feel like she has made a concerted effort over the years, and I appreciate it immensely."

The First Danger During the Power Struggle Stage

Conflicts eventually arise in any relationship because there are two unique individuals present. You want the thermostat set at seventy-three degrees; I want it at sixty-eight degrees. I say, "Put on a sweater if you're cold," and you say, "Take off your shirt if you're hot." The notion of extremes is important here. If I always give in to your way of doing things, I will gradually begin to lose my identity and disappear. If neither of us ever gives in, the resulting conflicts will be constant and, very likely, severe. When conflicts are constant and severe, the chances are good that the couple will be emotionally flooded a lot, which means their chances of using emotional nuclear weapons on each other is much too great.

Gottman showed that successful couples have ways of soothing themselves and their partner so that they don't flood very often. One woman put it this way: "My husband and I have a doozie of a fight every once in a while, and no matter how mad we are in the moment, and no matter how loud or intense we get, there is an executive part of each of us that stays in charge, so that we never seem to cross that line between loud anger and rageful contempt." When asked if she ever *thinks* hurtful things about her husband, she replied, "Of course I do. Everybody does. Haven't you ever been so mad at someone you love that you'd like to divorce him on the spot and run away, or worse, take all of the vulnerable things that you know about him from years of intimacy and clobber him with them? But if I did that, I'd destroy our relationship. And besides, he has as much history on me as I have on him. Our power is balanced in that respect. So we just don't let it escalate past anger."

Gottman identified what he called The Four Horsemen of the Apocalypse, which are the four things that harm a relationship the most. They are *criticism, contempt, defensiveness* and *stonewalling.* You might notice that two of them are active or "attack" strategies, while the other two are passive or "retreat" strategies. He has recently added a fifth, *belligerence.*[9] Gottman is very careful to distinguish between lodging a *complaint,* which is necessary in any relationship, to lobbing the bombs of criticism and contempt at your partner. It's one thing to say, "I'm really angry at you for being so late that we missed the opening act of the play." It's a very different and very damaging thing to say, "You're *always* late! What's *wrong* with you? I think you have a psychological problem. Why don't you go see a shrink and see if you can get straightened out?"

The Second Danger During the Power Struggle Stage

The second danger during this stage is that you *won't* have power struggles—at least not openly. You might ask, "What's the problem with not having power struggles?" The problem is that you remain in the Disneyland Existence of the early days of the relationship, which means your relationship remains shallow and unfulfilling. While occasionally a fun place to visit, Disneyland can get pretty monotonous in its incessant cleanliness and the constant drone of its manufactured cheer. The gouges on an old table or the discarded handbills drifting hypnotically down the street in the wind can make life interesting.

In a long-term relationship, the tugging and pulling and jockeying for position lets us know that, indeed, we are not alone in the universe. Equally important, these struggles prevent the boredom that can be one of the biggest of all relationship-killers. Routines and predictability are extremely important, as Catherine Johnson discovered in her research on healthy couples,[10] but layered beneath these routines is an ever-present awareness of and resonance with the unpredictable, fragile nature of life. The routines can be shattered at any moment. The ability to go with the direction of life's flow, and with our changing needs and desires within the relationship, keeps things fresh and alive even as we grow old and approach the end of life.

And so the next time you catch yourself bemoaning the fact that you and your partner seem to struggle with the same little things month after month, year after year, remember that the alternative could be worse. Your relationship could be turning into dust as the tedium and "niceness" grind the two of you into oblivion.

Stage IV: Hand-in-Hand

Simon and Garfunkel sang about old friends sitting on the park bench like bookends. There is something ineffable about two people who have been together for a long time and who have reached this stage. Not all couples get here. The *mutuality* that exists at this stage is hard to describe because it is filled with paradoxes and mysteries. By the time a couple reaches this point, there are so many discovered layers in themselves and in their relationship that describing it is like trying to describe a three-dimensional chess game with a snapshot. It really can't be done.

After all, how do I explain that the older and wiser I become, the freer I become, and yet the fewer choices I have because of it? How do I explain that I know you are the only one for me and that I'm the only one for you, and yet if one of us died, we would want the other to get out there and date? Research suggests that people who had really great marriages are the most likely to go right out and create another really great marriage, as opposed to the unhealthy marriages that are hastily put together out of dependency and neediness by some widows and widowers. How do I reconcile the fact that the older we get, and the closer to death we get, the more alive I feel, and the more complete I feel, the more palpable are the infinitesimal longings that I know will never be fulfilled, and the more exquisite the tiny regrets that have accumulated over the years?

Mutuality is walking hand-in-hand into the face of death without the paralyzing dread. It is missing each other when apart but not with a painful ache. It is the poignant savoring of every moment because of the personal knowledge that the moments cannot last forever. It is the sheer terror I felt when the doctors thought you had cancer, coupled with the solid conviction that we would get through it and endure, even if one of us died. It is noticing that you always leave the last quarter-inch of juice in the glass and then return it to the refrigerator, not giving it another thought. It is going to the mall with you while you look for a dress just because we enjoy each other's company, and then a little later, your willingness to tell me that I'm driving you crazy while we're there as I hover over you in the hopes that you'll make a selection sooner.

Mutuality is my suggesting we fly your son home for a spontaneous visit when he hits a big bump in the road, or you going out of your way to get a special birthday gift for my daughter. It's me not needing you to go in the ocean with me. It's you not needing me to be home at six o'clock every evening when my work requires me to be gone later than that. It's you going to that blow-'em-up movie with me even though you fall asleep as soon as the explosions and gunfire begin; or me reading that article in the travel section of the newspaper about cruises around the Greek islands. It's how we were both so deeply offended by the same political incident, and how we sometimes vote for different candidates but basically have very similar values when it comes to national and world affairs.

The paradox of mutuality is that, over the years, we have fought the good fights—engaged each other on the field of battle—sometimes with grace and honor, sometimes more clumsily. And now we face each other, neither one the winner nor loser. Rather than compromising ourselves out of existence for the sake of harmony—and that is the biggest danger during this stage—we create a much richer, deeper and more complicated harmony that is more like a five-dimensional chess game. On the surface, what might look like mindless capitulation to a naive observer is in fact the infinitely more subtle and more lovely act of *care with synchronization.*

Because I have experienced your woundedness and your "little-ness," which are wrapped in and supported by your grown-up strength and power, and simply because it is important to you, I *want* to go look at that model home with you. It is not a steely, disciplined act of my conscious will. It is a joyful desire of mine that can only be fulfilled by my accompanying you on your brief drive two neighborhoods north, in the middle of a bitterly cold snowstorm, to look at what turns out to be a delightful surprise for me.

Couples who agree on everything or compromise on everything without living out the process of struggling together and deepening together are still operating in a two-dimensional world. Not that it's a bad thing to do. It just isn't as complex. And because it isn't as complex, the world outside seems a great deal more perplexing than it does to the old friends, walking through the park, hand-in-hand, and stopping briefly to sit on the park bench like bookends.

7

We Always Pair Up
with Emotional Equals—And Other
Rules of the Game

In the end, one of the sentimental sensualities
turns into a passion—whether of longing
or disgust it matters not—and then,
farewell to all hope of tranquility.

—Aldous Huxley
Two or Three Graces

In a classic song, the singer wonders who penned the book
of love.

The answer? If there was a universal book on how to have
a good relationship, there wouldn't be such a big "relationships" section in most bookstores. And while there is as yet
no universal book on love, there do seem to be enough

principles that science has discovered to suggest a few pointers that you might find helpful. You may be quite familiar with some of these, and others not. So take what may be helpful, and leave the rest.

We Pair Up with People Whose Emotional Cups Are Filled to the Same Level As Ours

We put this first because many people get themselves stuck in the quagmire of actually believing that their long-term relationship partner is significantly more healthy or more "dysfunctional" than themselves. Notice that we emphasize *long-term relationship partner.* Part of the process of *dating* as opposed to *mating* is that in dating it is assumed that you will go out with people of many different emotional health levels. But as you get into the *mate-selection phase,* this variable balances out between the two partners. We have been presenting this information for years, and it still amazes a lot of people. Audience reaction ranges from nervous giggles of recognition to angry silence.

Think about it this way for a moment: Isn't it common for someone who grew up with a childhood history of abuse to marry someone who by all appearances had one of those "perfect" *Leave It to Beaver* childhoods? Many people ask how this could be, because the childhoods are so different. It is actually pretty simple, but mostly unconscious. Part of it has to do with overt dysfunction that we see easily versus covert dysfunction that is hidden from view. In the "perfect" *Leave It to Beaver* family, there may be many shortages that

we don't see easily. Dad and Mom could be overly protective, or too lax, or too strict. Everything could be in order
except that painful events aren't dealt with very well per
haps the family tries to ignore painful or confusing aspects
of life in the hopes that they will just go away. Every family
has its strengths and limitations.

Later in this chapter we discuss the rule that dysfunction
usually exists at the extremes. Psychologically, someone
who is *overly de*pendent is therefore just as dysfunctional as
one who is *overly in*dependent. The confusion often comes
because on some other measure, like financial health, they
may not be equal. An overly independent person may make
more money, or manage her money better, than an overly
dependent one. To continue with the above example, consider the partners who *have* paired up on this dimension. He
is overly dependent, and she is overly independent. If we use
the analogy of the "fuel" level in our emotional cups, then
these two people would be "low on fuel" in one area, as
shown in the left side of Figure 7.1.

Figure 7.1

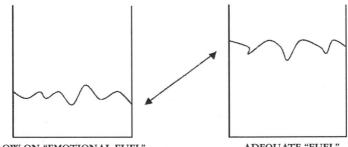

LOW ON "EMOTIONAL FUEL"   ADEQUATE "FUEL"
OVERLY INDEPENDENT OR   INTERDEPENDENT
OVERLY DEPENDENT

People do not pair up with emotional "unequals."
These two wouldn't get past the first couple of dates.

The first question we'd ask is, "What would happen if someone who was low on fuel went out on a date with a person whose cup was three-fourths full on this dimension, i.e., someone who had healthy *inter*dependence, also shown in Figure 7.1?" To answer this question, peruse the table below for a moment, which shows some of the shortages that stem from extremes on the dependency continuum, as well as what the healthy middle range looks like.

Overly Dependent	Interdependent	Overly Independent
Emotionally Clingy	Self-Reliant but Can Be Appropriately Vulnerable	Emotionally Distant, Blunted or Intellectualized
Asks for Help About Every Little Thing	Asks for Help When It Is Really Needed	Rarely, If Ever, Asks for Help
Is Desperate When Alone	Enjoys Times of Solitude	Feels As If S/He's Doing Life Alone
Emotions All over the Place	Emotions Both Expressed and Contained	Emotions Repressed and/or Intellectualized
Possibly Chemically Dependent	Healthy Soothing of Uncomfortable Feelings	Possibly Chemically Dependent
Passively Controlling or Manipulative	Competent	Controlling Dependent

Overly Dependent Person Dating Interdependent Person

You're a woman whose cup is three-fourths full on this dependency dimension. You are out on a first date with a man who is overly dependent. You are very attracted to each other. You have some things in common. You both have good initial social skills. At the end of the date, which was very nice, he asks if he can see you again. Your heart flutters for a second. "Yes," you say. "I'd love to. But I'm going away on a business trip and won't be back until the following Monday. Could it be in two weeks?" The man's face shows an infinitesimal trace of a wince, but without missing a beat, he arches his head back an inch or two and says with an equally small trace of sarcasm in his voice, "Oh. Out of town? Are you work-addicted or something?" *Ouch,* you say to yourself. *That was way out of line. My stomach just went into a knot and my breathing stopped for a second. Hmmm. I need to take my time with this.*

Of course, the rest is history. He sensed your pause and knew that he'd sent a barb across the table, and if he'd been healthier, he would have said, "I shouldn't have said that. That was unfair. I think I felt a little threatened because I'd like to see you again and for a second I feared the worst— you know, that you'd fly off into the sunset and I'd never see you again. I apologize."

To which you could have said, quite relieved now, "Oh. I do this trip twice a year. I'd like to see you again, too."

To which he could have said, "Great. Have a good trip."

But he didn't.

Overly Independent Person Dating Interdependent Person

You're a man whose cup is three-fourths full, and you're on your first date with a woman who is overly independent. You're very attracted to each other, and you have a number of things in common. As the evening progresses, the nascent chemistry that was there earlier begins to wane. You're puzzled. *Is it me?* you ask yourself. *Maybe I'm tired. It's been a long day.* You pay attention to the flow of conversation back and forth, while noticing your reactions. *We're in sync on politics, that's for sure,* you say to yourself. *We both loved that latest Spielberg film, and for the same reasons. What is it? I can't put my finger on it.*

She tells you about the big project she is working on for her company's largest account, and she is animated and intense. *That's good. She's passionate about her life,* you think. She shares some of the painful things that happened when she was growing up but is appropriate with containing the details on a first date, and sums it up by saying she's worked them through and is glad for that. That shows balance and poise and . . . it all sounds so . . . so complete. *That's it. It all sounds so complete. Hmmm. What's wrong with that?* you ask yourself. The evening continues. It is pleasant, interesting, engaging, fun. It was a good date. You agree to meet again next Saturday night. You drop her off at her house, give her a peck on the cheek, and say, "Goodnight."

As you fall asleep that night, you can't get her out of your mind, but not because you're head-over-heels in love. It's more because something isn't quite right, and you don't know what. You fall asleep thinking, *I'll have to sleep on this.* And so you do. When you awaken the next morning, you realize you had a dream, although you can't quite remember the details. But there is a lingering sense of comfort drifting into consciousness as a result of it. This woman is very nice and very accomplished and very kind and very intelligent and very passionate about her life. We haven't "connected" yet. *That's all I know,* you tell yourself.

On your next date, she hops into the car and pats you on the arm quickly and says how much fun she had the other evening. She is bubbly and animated again. She asks how your week was. You start to tell her, and then she jumps in and tells you about a new kind of meditation that she just read about. You say it sounds interesting and tell her that you do some meditation most every day. She asks, "Most every day?" You answer, "Yes, probably four to five days a week, depending." She asks why you couldn't do it every day, and before you answer, she tells you why it would be better if you did it every day. You feel your stomach go into a knot and your breathing stop for a second. You don't want to get defensive. That just blocks intimacy. So you say cheerfully, "I'll have to think about that. Thanks." She moves closer to you as you drive toward the restaurant, and you feel yourself back off a little bit.

Perhaps you have never read a self-help book, so you may not have the terminology to attach to this, but if we could whisper in your ear right now, we'd suggest that you may be on a date with a person who is what we call *controlling-dependent.* It's confusing, because in one sense it looks like confidence and competence. At another level, it's an attempt to make you be and do the same as me, so I don't have to fear your separateness from me. If you not only like to meditate, but like the same kind of meditation as I do, and do it with the same frequency, then we're the same and I feel safe. Furthermore, if I can focus on fixing you (even though you don't need to be fixed), then I can have the illusion of safety, because if I control you, you won't ever hurt me. Plus, if I focus on fixing you, I can avoid looking at myself. And if you ever suggest that I'm controlling, I can run through scores of reasons why I'm not, and each one, by itself, will sound perfectly reasonable. It's quite a sticky wicket.

This rule is often a painful one to digest. We listed it as the most important rule of the game because to fully grasp it and all of its nuances means that you are on the threshold of growing up and assuming responsibility for yourself in the relationship—and more importantly—in the world. So if you catch yourself saying, "I will be happy in this relationship when *she* decides to change," go the next step and tell yourself, "Oops! That's a sign! What can *I* do to become a healthier person in this relationship?"

Paradoxically, It Isn't 50/50

Our discussion above refers to an overall measure of emotional maturity and emotional health. If you and your partner are both three-fourths full, then you're in good shape. But no matter how much we grow and how healthy we get, we're still human, and therefore we still have limitations. So when there is a "problem" in the relationship—something that is causing distress and conflict and struggle—is it always a 50/50 proposition? No.

If I have a problem with my back, it is my problem. It certainly affects you at times, but all-in-all, it's an 80/20 proposition. It's my back, and therefore it's my problem. What might your 20 percent be? Maybe you hover over me too much instead of letting me handle it myself. Or maybe you're too insensitive about it. Maybe you nag me to go see the doctor after I just got back from the doctor, and there's nothing more anyone can do for the time being. So, there are things you could do to help reduce the distress or conflict in our household related to my back problem, but the majority of responsibility and effort at managing the problem is mine.

If you are physically abusive, the majority of the problem is yours, because there simply is no excuse for physical abuse. My part may be that I keep staying in the relationship naively hoping that "this time will be the last time that you hit me." Or my part could be that I have so little real emotional support outside of our relationship, that just the thought of leaving to protect my own safety produces paralyzing fear. So while you're attending a domestic-violence program, I might want to get myself into a women's therapy group so that I can start filling up my cup, too. But the majority of the problem of your physically abusing me is your problem, not mine.

Relationships Have Ever-Deepening Levels, and a Relationship Can Only Go to the Depth of the More Limited Person

Levels of "Self"

As you look at Figure 7.2, think about your own development over the years. We use this drawing to represent the ever-deepening layers of each person's psyche or "self." The more emotional depth (maturity) that we have, the richer and more complex is our experience of life, and at the same time, the simpler life becomes. This paradox helps explain a lot of seemingly contradictory "facts." For example, if you are only able to function at a surface level because going any deeper would dredge up too much discomfort, then life will be simpler in one way—everything will be black and white. There will be good guys in white hats and bad guys in black hats. It will be easy to judge who's a saint and who's a sinner. And, you'll very likely do a lot of judging of others along the way.

Figure 7.2

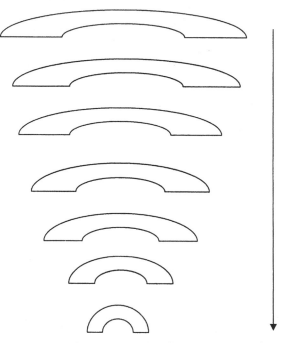

The deeper you go towards your "core self," the richer and more complex life becomes, and the easier it gets to comprehend life and make sense out of it.

Psychologists have known for decades that having an *authoritarian personality*—being rigid, intolerant of differences, always having to be right, and being mean to subordinates while licking the boots of your superiors—is not a very happy or peaceful way to live.[11] If you always need to be right and are frightened and intolerant of people who are different, you may be struggling in the shallow end of the pool. That is what life is like when we can't get deeper than the surface of our own being.

Operating a few layers down, people realize that life is so much more complex and subtle than just white hats and black hats. They will still have strong moral positions and clear boundaries in certain areas of life, so don't think of this as a blur of gray—as nothing more than moral relativism. But accepting the uncontrollable in life, and their own humanity, allows them to accept and better understand many of the confusing flaws in the world. How can such great men as Dwight D. Eisenhower and Franklin D. Roosevelt have extramarital affairs? How do we reconcile those facts with our notions of greatness? How could Churchill have been a drunk? I don't have to condone having an extramarital affair to also say that these were great men. All I have to do is to say these are great men who, like all of us, had flaws, and that I am glad this is not one of my flaws.

Levels of Intimacy

We often have conversations much like the abbreviated one that follows. A person says, "I want a deeper relationship than she is capable of having. What can I do about it?"

Of course, the answer is, "Nothing."

"But what if I bring her along . . . you know . . . I'm significantly healthier than she is, so if I stay in the relationship with her and become her mentor, can't I eventually get her to where she's my emotional equal?"

"She already is your emotional equal if you believe you can do what you just said."

"Huh?"

Healthy adults know that they can't make someone else have a relationship at a deeper level than the other person is capable of having. This leads to the helpful conclusion, frightening at first, that *whatever two adults can give each other at the time is enough.* The implications of this little quote are far-reaching. On the one hand, it means that if we're both equally healthy, but you aren't in love with me, although I am with you, then what you can give me—friendship, casual acquaintanceship or nothing—will be enough for me. I will have to be able to go on and flourish with that as it is.

On the other hand, it may mean that you are significantly healthier than I, and so being, you realize that your relationship with me will be severely curtailed because of my limitations. And so you are content to have the relationship that you can have with me instead of pining away for the one you can't have with me because I'm not able to have it. This is especially important in relationships between parents and children or between siblings of different health levels. It is such a relief for our clients when they stop trying to have a "deep, meaningful relationship" with their eighty-three-year-old parents who went through the Depression and World War II and who have never had the luxury of digging through their interior psychological spaces because they've been trying to make ends meet ever since.

Extremes Almost Always Equal Dysfunction

Picture a needle gauge that, rather than being round, is straight, linear. It has gradations on it, and at one end it says "Never," and at the other end, it says "Always." In the middle area, which takes up about a third of the gauge, it says "Sometimes." The needle can travel freely, back and forth between the two extremes. Our job as evolving human beings is to try to keep the needle in the fairly wide middle area as much as possible, always mindful that perfection is not an option. The goal is to do a good job of it based on where we're starting from, knowing that if we could always do it perfectly, we wouldn't be human beings.

Figure 7.3

NEVER   SOMETIMES   ALWAYS

Just about everyone who has ever worked with us as a client of any kind knows how much importance we put on the skill of *staking out the extremes.* Whether they are parents wanting advice on how to be better parents, individuals trying to overcome depression, court-ordered clients who have problems controlling their tempers, recovering alcoholics or addicts, corporate executives wondering how to manage their employees better, or teachers and psycho-therapists wanting to know how to be more effective in their work, we always end up coming back around to the importance of staking out the extremes. What we have dis-covered is that the more severe or intense the person's prob-lem, the more valuable it is to do this, too.

We call the ability to stake out the extremes *The Universal Skill* because it is unquestionably and pervasively useful at all ages and across all cultures and belief systems. There are few circumstances where this ability to locate the ends of a continuum, and then the middle range in between, is not of the utmost utility. And there are many times when it is life-saving.

Setting the Stakes in the Ground

A helpful exercise we do when trying to sort something out, or that we ask our clients to do when there is confusion about what is "right" or "healthy," is to first draw a line across a piece of paper and then create a scale using the line:

Figure 7.4

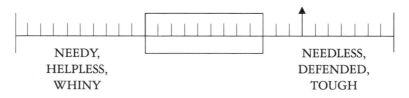

NEEDY,	NEEDLESS,
HELPLESS,	DEFENDED,
WHINY	TOUGH

Then we ask them to give a few examples of these, because people sometimes understand things in the abstract but have a hard time translating that into concrete, real-life terms. We might ask, "How would I know if someone were being needy, helpless and whiny?" You might answer with, "I had a friend last year who couldn't make any decisions for himself, and when things didn't go his way, he complained and groaned and moaned about it to anyone who'd listen to him. And he'd ask for help with things he should be able to do himself, like iron his shirts or cook a meal."

We might then ask, "And what would it look like if someone were 'need*less*'?" One man replied, "My cousin is like that. He not only won't ever ask for directions, but he won't ask for help doing his taxes, fixing his car or operating his computer. The poor guy spent two entire weekends trying to untangle a software mess on his computer by himself, and then on Monday afternoon while he was at work, his sixteen-year-old son finally called tech support at Gateway and had it figured out in thirty-five minutes! What a waste." He gave another example as he went on to describe his mother as a woman who "lets everyone lean on her for emotional support and advice—people are calling her at all hours of the day and night—but she swears she doesn't have anyone she can lean on when things are tough for her. She does, but she just won't let herself be vulnerable with anyone."

Fill In the Middle

Then we ask people to try filling in the middle. You might say, "Hmmmm. The middle. Well, it would be like someone who is open and available to others, you know, lets his defenses down sometimes, and yet one who is self-reliant and independent. He would ask for help when he needed it, without sounding helpless and inept. He would be able and willing to help others, but not all the time. Not night and day. He would put some reasonable limits on how much he took from others and on how much he gave to others. Let's see. What else? He'd be capable of getting emotionally close to others, and he could tolerate and enjoy others being close to him. He'd probably be seen as strong but warm and open."

At this point we might jot down the word "interdependent" and then tell our client that he's done a very good job of defining the extreme ends of this continuum, and of mapping the middle ground as well. As people do this exercise over and over again, they report that subtle changes begin

Figure 7.5

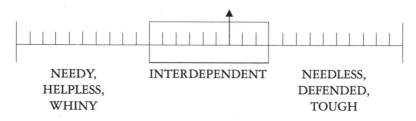

NEEDY,   INTERDEPENDENT   NEEDLESS,
HELPLESS,   DEFENDED,
WHINY   TOUGH

to take place inside of them. For example, when a friend says something troubling to you, you may feel a sting but may not blow it out of proportion, as in: "When Bob said he thought I was making a big mistake for taking that new job, I felt really bad. I didn't like what he said. But, I guess we can continue to be friends for now, *and* I'm very glad that I took that new job. I love it, and I'm making a small fortune, too." When people become conversant with the extremes and the middle between them, they find their reactions to things are more balanced. They find themselves less troubled by life's challenges, and they find that they hurt themselves and others less often.

When you look at everything in black-and-white, either-or terms, it can certainly make for an exciting news story. It can create a lot of drama and hype. People often feel energized when operating in the extremes. Of course, if you assume that the average American isn't bright enough to grasp the subtlety and richness of life, then looking at everything in the extremes is the way to go. And while some people believe that having a balanced, moderate response to life is boring, it's actually a far cry from boring. In fact, when we think of extreme responses, a few of the images that come to mind include "crude," "unrefined," "lacking subtlety," "lacking finesse," "tactless" and "artless."

Imagine how much effort and struggle it takes a man or woman to learn enough about art, music or astrophysics in order to have the deepest appreciation possible for a painting, symphony or an event a million light years out in the universe. You might rightfully argue that one needs no education in order to appreciate these things, which is why we appended the modifier "deepest" in the sentence above. Remember, too, that education includes "education of the senses," as in learning to discern and appreciate the differences between fine coffees or the fragrances of tropical flowers.

Because we've found it so useful to be able to discern the boundaries of the extremes and the location of the middle ground, we will list a few more examples below, which can be added to the extremes mentioned in the section above on "choosing partners of equal emotional health." There are many more, but these should give you an idea of what we're talking about.

- Permissive, lax parenting vs. Strict, rigid parenting
- Lax or nonexistent religious or spiritual training vs. Rigid or strict religious or spiritual training
- Helping others too much vs. Caring for no one but yourself
- Taking few risks vs. Taking excessive risks
- Compulsive cleaning or neatness vs. Being a terrible slob
- All work, no play vs. Putting no energy into work
- Crying all the time vs. Never crying
- Always following the rules vs. Hardly ever following any of the rules
- Never daydreaming vs. Always daydreaming
- Saving compulsively vs. Spending compulsively
- Victim vs. Perpetrator

In closing this section with a favorite quote from John Steinbeck's *Cannery Row,* we are reminded how simple and complex we human beings are, and how important it is to transcend the polar opposites of life:

> *Its inhabitants are, as the man once said, "Whores, pimps, gamblers, and sons of bitches, by which he meant everybody." Had the man looked through another peephole, he might have said, "Saints and angels and martyrs and holy men," and he would have meant the same thing.*[12]

Small Changes Yield Big Results

One change instituted consistently can turn an entire system around. Think about one of our space probes just leaving Earth's orbit on its way to Jupiter. Imagine it being off course by a fraction of a degree. Now, imagine Mission Control officials being unable to make this tiny midcourse correction because of a malfunction in the probe's thrusters. Lastly, imagine where the probe will be, several years later, when it is supposed to be entering Jupiter's atmosphere. That's right. It will be millions of miles off course by then. Small changes yield big results.

Sometimes people enter therapy looking for high drama and quick fixes. Sometimes people seek the magic bullet that will change their entire life overnight. In so doing, people miss the fact that one small change, maintained consistently and with integrity, can indeed change an entire system. Of course, systemic change won't happen overnight, no matter what you do, which means that before we can truly grow, we must embrace the ordinary as well as the enduring in life.

We have found it helpful to suggest that people visualize a dial with a 360-degree scale on it and with a strong spring inside that tries to keep the dial at 0 degrees. Imagine yourself cranking that dial clockwise 270 degrees and then letting it go. We all know what happens shortly after this "change." Business as usual.

Now imagine turning that dial 7 degrees and holding it there for twelve months despite the strong spring inside the dial that is trying to pull it back to 0. After twelve months of working diligently to keep it at 7 degrees, you let go of the dial and find that it stays at 7 degrees—the spring inside has adjusted to the new setting. Furthermore, you discover that many other aspects of your life have changed in important ways because of the internal growth that took place as you chose to work patiently to achieve this success instead of going for the quick fix.

We Pick Partners Who Have the Worst Traits of Our Parents for a Very Positive Reason

Harville Hendrix[13] made this fascinating insight one of the cornerstones of his Imago Therapy®. While partner choice is a very complex process, we do pick partners based partially on the characteristics of the people we grow up with and who therefore were our first love experiences. When someone says, "You're just like my mother or father!" there will be some truth to it. So why would we do something so counterintuitive as to pick the very person we vowed we would never pick? Hendrix suggested that we do so because it then affords us the unique opportunity to heal old wounds, without doing the impossible feat of going back and reliving our childhoods.

If you go back and reread chapter 4, The Man, the Woman and the Sea, this should make perfect sense. The difference between literally marrying someone *just like* your father or mother, as opposed to someone who is *not exactly* like him or her, is that by growing up yourself, and struggling with your partner, you have a good opportunity for the two of you to change those traits *just enough* to make the whole ball game different. You may be gruff and grumpy, but if you're also willing to be fair and own your part in things and apologize at times, and accept who I am even though it sometimes disappoints you, then we each heal those old, old wounds, from the inside out.

Reenactment Is a Given

We *will* replay the major functional as well as painful aspects of our childhoods, at least in our twenties and very often well beyond, no matter how strongly we believe otherwise. Each person will typically do this in such a way that he will be almost completely oblivious to it—he will be convinced that he has moved beyond early painful patterns because it is in his nature to do it this way. We discuss this point in various ways throughout this book, but thought it important enough to have a special listing in this chapter.

Emotions Need to Be
Both Expressed and Contained

People who believe that their emotions should be both expressed and routinely *acted* upon are at very high risk for doing irreparable harm to their partners and ruining their romantic relationships. Yes, emotions need to be expressed. There can be no emotional connection between people without it. But emotions also need to be *contained* at times, too.

The belief that "If I feel it, I should act on it" is a dangerous one unless it is also tempered by a parallel belief that "I must evaluate which feelings to express and which ones to contain." Otherwise, we are nothing more than wild animals acting out our primitive impulses all the time.

It is human nature to hurt the people closest to us, as in "We only hurt the ones we love." Our greatest investments and our greatest potential for losses are with those to whom we are closest. But the people who are unable to rise above this aspect of our human nature will continue to have troubled or broken relationships until they change this pattern. In other words, we are responsible for our emotions and for how we choose to act on them. Just because we *believe* that what we say or do isn't hurting anyone does not mean that it is fine. It is quite common to hurt people and think we're "just kidding," when in fact we're "just hurting" the person.

READER/CUSTOMER CARE SURVEY

We care about your opinions. Please take a moment to fill out this Reader Survey card and mail it back to us.
As a special "thank you" we'll send you exciting news about interesting books and a valuable **Gift Certificate.**

Please PRINT using ALL CAPS

First Name |__|__|__|__|__|__|__|__|__|__|__| MI. |__| Last Name |__|__|__|__|__|__|__|__|__|__|

Address |__|__|__|__|__|__|__|__|__|__|__|__|__|__|__|__|__|__|__|__|

City |__|__|__|__|__|__|__|__|__|__|__| ST |__|__| Zip |__|__|__|__|__| — |__|__|__|__|

Phone # (|__|__|__|) |__|__|__| — |__|__|__|__| Fax # (|__|__|__|) |__|__|__| — |__|__|__|__|

Email |__|__|__|__|__|__|__|__|__|__|__|__|__|__|__|__|__|__|__|__|

(1) Gender:
___ Female   ___ Male

(2) Age:
___ 12 or under   ___ 40-59
___ 13-19   ___ 60+
___ 20-39

(3) Marital Status
___ Married
___ Single
___ Divorced/Widowed

(4) Did you receive this book as a gift?
___ Yes   ___ No

(5) How many Health Communications books have you bought or read?
___ 1   ___ 2-4   ___ 5+

(6) How did you find out about this book?
Please fill in ONE.
1) ___ Recommendation
2) ___ Store Display
3) ___ Bestseller List
4) ___ Online
5) ___ Advertisement
6) ___ Catalog/Mailing
7) ___ Interview/Review (TV, Radio, Print)

(7) Where do you usually buy books?
Please fill in your top TWO choices.
1) ___ Bookstore
2) ___ Religious Bookstore
3) ___ Online
4) ___ Book Club/Mail Order
5) ___ Price Club (Costco, Sam's Club, etc.)
6) ___ Retail Store (Target, Wal-Mart, etc.)

(9) What subjects do you enjoy reading about most? Rank only *FIVE.* Use 1 for your favorite, 2 for second favorite, etc.

	1	2	3	4	5
1) Parenting/Family	○	○	○	○	○
2) Relationships	○	○	○	○	○
3) Recovery/Addictions	○	○	○	○	○
4) Health/Nutrition	○	○	○	○	○
5) Christianity	○	○	○	○	○
6) Spirituality/Inspiration	○	○	○	○	○
7) Business Self-Help	○	○	○	○	○
8) Teen Issues	○	○	○	○	○
9) Sports	○	○	○	○	○

(14) What attracts you most to a book?
(Please rank 1-4 in order of preference.)

	1	2	3	4
1) Title	○	○	○	○
2) Cover Design	○	○	○	○
3) Author	○	○	○	○
4) Content	○	○	○	○

TAPE IN MIDDLE; DO NOT STAPLE

BUSINESS REPLY MAIL
FIRST-CLASS MAIL PERMIT NO 45 DEERFIELD BEACH, FL

POSTAGE WILL BE PAID BY ADDRESSEE

HEALTH COMMUNICATIONS, INC.
3201 SW 15TH STREET
DEERFIELD BEACH FL 33442-9875

I₁ll₁₁ll₁d₁l₁ll₁l₁l₁ldll₁l₁l₁l₁₁l₁ldl₁l₁l₁l

FOLD HERE

Comments:

Part III

"And" Is a Powerful Word

I caught his face in my hands . . . and I held it like that. And it was such a strange sensation—I must have never touched his face before—is that possible never to have touched my father's face? And it seemed so small between my hands; and it was so cool and his beard so rough and I felt so—so equal to him (she begins to cry).

Brian Friel
Aristocrats

8

The Rocks

And yet here we all were. The city was once
again being repaired and prepared, and the gentle
weather seemed to promise that God
had not meant it after all.

—Peter Theroux
Translating L.A.

Once upon a time there was a little boy who lived on a
lake near a small town in the far North Woods of
Minnesota, near the Canadian border. The little boy loved
the lake more than anything in the world. The lake fed the
family, cooled his fevered brow on a sweltering summer day
and soothed his spirit on a lonely, sad fall afternoon when
he didn't know if the sun would ever shine brightly again.

There were troubles in the little boy's home, and he
struggled hard to make sense of them. When he was very

young, five maybe, he awoke to screaming and the shattering of glass in the middle of the night. He rubbed his sleepy eyes and tried to focus them as he peered into the living room from his vantage point behind the plain, narrow staircase that his father and mother climbed each night on their way to bed. His heart pounded, and his hands were sweaty. There was a lump in his throat that almost felt like the choking hands of a grown man. He was so scared—that his parents would hurt each other, scared that they might accidentally hurt him, scared that one of them might leave and never return, scared that the neighbors might call the police, scared that somebody in his house might die.

When he was seven, he found himself sitting by the lake one afternoon, the early summer sun warming the back of his neck and shoulders at the same time that a breath of cool air from the northwest brushed by his forehead on its way south. He felt sad and empty. It was a hollow feeling, like the bowels of an empty cavern. He knew what it was. He felt lonely. He felt scared. Together, these feelings created an ache in his gut and a vacancy in his chest that were almost more than he could bear, but not quite. They were so familiar to the daily rhythms of his life that he bore them with barely a wince.

When he was ten years old, this little boy came home from school one day with his report card in one hand, a small paper bag of rocks in the other and a smile on his face that could warm the heart of the coldest soul. "I got all As," he shouted. "It's the first time!" His father, looking sullen and unhappy, looked over at him as if he were a stray dog, caught sight of the bag of rocks, and grumbled, "What's that you have there?"

"Some interesting rocks I found down by the lake, on the other side, near that big dying birch tree."

His father grabbed the paper bag from the boy's poised hands, peered inside and said with a snicker, "What's so interesting about these rocks? There's nothing special about them at all. You want rocks? Here, I'll show you rocks." The man ushered his son behind the house and marched him into the woods for a hundred yards, where someone had been digging up large rocks and piling them next to a tall pine tree. "Here," he continued. "I'm digging up these rocks and stacking them there so we can eventually build a stone wall around our land."

"What for?" the boy asked.

"What for?" the man asked with a sarcastic, teasing tone of voice. "You ask so many questions. Don't you think I know what I'm doing?"

"Yes, Father. I think you know what you're doing. I was just wondering why."

"It's good to have a wall around your land. It says where your land is, so there's no mistaking it."

"I see," the boy said.

"You're old enough to help. Throw out that little bag of stones and start digging up these rocks. C'mon. It won't be dark for another two hours. Get to work."

The little boy stayed behind with a pick and shovel, working diligently, as his father disappeared into the woods, heading toward the house. The rocks were big. He could barely roll them over to the tall pine tree, let alone carry them. He labored ceaselessly until the sun descended behind the horizon and a North Woods chill began to seep into his bones, and then he stopped. *I wonder why my father didn't ask me about my report card,* he said to himself as he carried the pick and shovel back to the house and went in for dinner.

A few days later, while he was digging up boulders, his father came out to the place where the tall pine tree stood and said, "You want to carry a sack of rocks around? Okay. I have an idea that will help to make a man out of you. I want you to carry some rocks in this knapsack."

"Where to?" the boy asked.

"Everywhere you go," his father replied. "You go to school and get good grades, but if you don't learn the bigger lessons in life, you'll never make it. So I want you to start carrying this knapsack full of rocks wherever you go. It will make you strong."

The boy felt sick. It made no sense. It was as if his father had suddenly stepped across the boundary from unhappiness to derangement. But he was only ten. There was little he could do. So he picked up the knapsack and hoisted it onto his back, adjusting the straps so they wouldn't dig into his shoulders so much. He quickly became resigned to his plight, dutifully hoisting the knapsack of large, jagged rocks onto his back every morning and dumping it next to his bed every night. His father said nothing more about the rocks, and soon it became a part of the daily rhythms of life along the lake in the North Woods of Minnesota. But he kept saying to himself, day after day after day, *I hate my father, I hate the lake, I hate school, I hate the North Woods. And someday I will leave this place, throw away this sack of rocks and never return!*

One day it was time for him to leave. He was very confused. He didn't hate the North Woods. He didn't hate school. He didn't hate the lake. He wasn't even sure he hated his father. He just knew it was time to leave. He couldn't even leave the sack of rocks behind. As he boarded the early morning bus headed "to all points south and west," he lugged that knapsack of large, jagged rocks up the stairs of the bus and back to his seat, dropping them with a deep thud on the seat next to him. He cried and cried and cried and cried, and then just when he thought he was done crying, he cried some more. The bus lumbered on and on. He slept. He awoke at a stop, got a bite to eat, went back to his seat, and slept and slept. He told himself that he would stop when the time was right. When he awoke again, it was late afternoon. The sunset on the prairie was the most magnificent thing he had ever seen. He was stunned by its beauty. And then it was over as suddenly as it began.

He rode for many more hours, days it seemed, as the bus turned south and droned on, until he awoke to a sunrise that took his breath away. The landscape was an infinite array of browns and reds and pastels of pink and orange, punctuated by sagebrush and cactus and sand. The sand spread out in front of him farther than the wheat on the prairie. He was in the desert. He knew it was time to stop. When the bus pulled into the station in Tucson, he disembarked, lugging his duffel bag of clothes and belongings just inches above the ground, the knapsack of rocks pulling relentlessly on his shoulders. He found a job and a place to stay, and the next day he enrolled in school.

Four years later, he graduated with honors. He went to

work. He knew how to work. He dazzled them. Everyone. He took care of himself. He ran every day. He learned to enjoy fine coffees and wines but always in moderation. He bought a house. As the contents of the rented truck poured into his new garage and found their way into the house, he stumbled onto the old, ratty, tattered, dirty knapsack. He yanked at it and abruptly stopped. *The rocks,* he said to himself. *Careful. Don't tear your arm out of its socket.* He carefully hoisted the knapsack up and off the dusty floor of the truck and carried it into the garage.

"I have to . . ." He paused and stared down at the old knapsack. ". . . I have to get rid of this." He felt a deep sadness come over him, but it was like the gentle swirling of breeze-blown musty lace curtains rather than a tidal wave. He felt that hollow feeling and that loneliness. Then the ache in his gut returned, followed by the vacancy in his chest. The rocks in the knapsack and the lake and his father and mother and the Minnesota North Woods and his school all fused together in an amalgam that was too complex to reconcile. He dragged the old knapsack behind the house, and then dragged it a hundred yards to the south and buried it near a grand old saguaro cactus.

Over the ensuing months, he made his new house a home. He decorated it carefully, expressing his personality as he understood it at the time. He started his own business. He met a woman and fell in love. They wanted a home that represented both of them, and the lot to the south was available. It had one large saguaro cactus on the property. His wife began to design the home while he poured his heart and soul into the business. The home she built and

decorated filled his heart with joy and peace. Each detail
was either an expression of her deep spirit or a subtle part of
him. He wondered how she could know him that way.

They had their first child. His business flourished. His
child grew. His marriage deepened. And then one day he
found himself irritated with his five-year-old son. He was
ashamed of his feelings. They scared him. He apologized to
his son for snapping at him. That night, he wandered out
into the desert to reflect on his life. They had built their
house about one hundred yards south of the grand old
saguaro cactus, and as he followed the North Star while
engrossed in his troubled musings, he found himself standing next to it. He sat down on the desert floor and felt his
eyes mercifully fill with tears. It wasn't the uncontrollable
sobbing that he'd experienced on the bus, years ago. It was
gentler and deeper. He looked up at the stars, then at the
silhouette of the cactus against the night sky. He picked up
a sharp stone and began tracing circles in the sand. And
then he started digging.

A few days later, while he was searching for something on
the Internet, his wife appeared behind him and rested her
hand on his shoulder, affectionately. He looked up, slightly
startled, appreciating the intimate intrusion into his
focused intensity, and said, "I'm not sure what this is about,
but ever since you've made this home for us out here in this
enigmatic desert, I've been haunted by images of rocks."

She felt wonder and anticipation as she rubbed his shoulder and replied, "Rocks."

"Rocks." He chuckled nervously. "I don't know. When I
first moved to Arizona, I was enchanted by the desert. I was

enchanted by the play of light on the rocks and the nuances of sun on sand. It drew me in. I was spellbound. I stayed. I had no choice."

"No choice. I think I understand. I felt that way when I met you," she said.

He was startled again. "Yes. That's it. I felt that way." He was so in love with her, but so anxious. It was more than he could apprehend. "I don't know," he repeated. "I've been enchanted by rocks." He gathered himself. "I think there's a hobby here. An avocation. A way to relax. The business has been so intense. I can teach our son. And make you some jewelry!" he exclaimed, like a child.

"Rocks are solid," she said wisely. "They endure. They connect deeply into the Earth."

"Yes," he replied, as she brushed her hand across his back and went off to put their son to bed.

♥ ♥ ♥

Six weeks later, on a Saturday morning, she returned from her long morning walk with their dog and heard a grinding noise coming from the garage. When she came up behind him he was admiring what must have been a finished product, judging by the gleam in his eye.

"Rocks?" she playfully asked.

"A polished one," he replied. "Small. Just a glimmer of its former self. But more than it ever was before, too. Like love."

"It's beautiful." She was taken by it. "Where did it come from?"

"From there," he said, pointing north. "Up by that old cactus."

"It's so beautiful," she said again, mystified.

"I knew there was something about rocks," he said. "I just didn't know what."

"Well, you got it right."

He felt.

Four months later, as they walked with their son and the dog, they happened by the grand old saguaro cactus, and she stopped. "Look. It looks like someone has been digging."

He wasn't anxious. He didn't feel the least bit cornered. "That's where I got the rocks."

"The rocks. Yes. Of course," she said. "That's where you got the rocks. It's such a beautiful place . . . by this grand old cactus . . . so near our home."

"That's what's so wonderful about it," he said, excitedly, like a child.

♥ ♥ ♥

Two years later, the day before their tenth wedding anniversary, after they put their son to bed and were settling in for an evening to themselves, he was finishing up the dishes. She was cleaning up the family room. It suddenly dawned on him. Tears started to roll down his cheeks. They kept coming, comfortably. She came through the kitchen to take some trash to the garage and noticed his tears. She stopped.

"The rocks," he began. "I want you to know about the rocks."

"I'd like that," she said.

He shook. He felt ashamed and angry. He wept. Compassion came, followed by understanding. She listened. He described the lake in exquisite detail, sharing every inch of its shore with her. She wasn't surprised that he had earned excellent grades, but she was proud. Hours later, as he described how frustrated and confused he was about burying the knapsack out in the desert by the grand old saguaro cactus, she wept, too. It was getting pretty close to home. "I finally discovered that you can love someone and hate them at the same moment in time," he cried.

♥ ♥ ♥

Years later, his grandson asked about that little satchel of fine Spanish leather, filled with six beautiful, highly polished stones. He told him that he wasn't sure he could ever explain it, but he'd try. As they passed the tall pine tree, his grandson smiled, looking forward to their warm conversation at the cabin by the lake in the Minnesota North Woods, and at that very moment, back in Arizona, his wife's heart filled.

Part IV

Seven (Plus One) Is a Good Round Number

Artemis loved the healing sound of rain—the sound of all running water—brooks, gutters, spouts, falls, and taps. . . . Men sought water as water sought its level. The pursuit of water accounted for epochal migrations. Man was largely water. Water was man. Water was love. Water was water.

John Cheever
Artemis, The Honest Well Digger

9

Grow Up: You Can't Be Married If You're Not Old Enough to Date

I could not have understood at this age of course,
only eight or nine, what it might mean to have a
voice one day, to speak as a writer speaks. I would
have been baffled by the thought.

—Barry Lopez
About This Life

Several years ago in a therapy session, a man was talking about what turned out to be a string of disappointing relationships with a common pattern—a good beginning, a frustrating period of feeling like his needs were not being met, followed by weeks or months of intractable conflict, all leading to an eventual breakup of the relationship. He spoke of his new girlfriend and how upset and angry he would become with her. "My needs are not getting met," he lamented.

"You can't be married if you aren't old enough to date" was the reply that spontaneously popped out of our mouths. It was said with genuine warmth, and the man did a subtle double-take. Months later, he marked that day as the day he began to move toward "relationship sanity."

It is a tough reality to face. But it explains a lot. And once you admit it, you can do something about it. If you are so terrified of losing your lover to another man that you hire a private investigator to constantly follow her around, then you either need to end the relationship because it's a bad one, or you need to grow up, because you can't be that afraid of abandonment and have a good relationship!

If you are so unclear about your own identity that you find yourself beginning a string of extramarital affairs a year into your marriage, then it's time to ask yourself why you got married in the first place, and what it will take for you to be in a monogamous relationship.

Being old enough to date means that you have enough of an internal *emotional skeleton* to sustain the weight of adult relationships. If your internal emotional structure is so brittle or so mushy that it can't hold you up, then it's time to get some help. In adult relationships, you don't get everything you want. Even if you're really, really scared, you can't expect the other person to always be there. What if he is away on business? Do you rage at him when you finally reach him that night, punishing him "for scaring you" and "for being so inconsiderate," or do you learn to soothe yourself and rely on other support in his absence?

Are you so self-centered that everything is about *you*? Can you take another's point of view? Can you see the impact of your behavior on others? Can you feel shame and not get so overwhelmed by it that you have to dump it on those around you? Can you admit when you are wrong? On the flip side, can you stand up for yourself when the chips are down? Are you willing to go toe-to-toe and head-to-head with your partner when you feel your integrity or identity is on the line, or that you will become invisible if you don't?

Togetherness is a good thing. Separateness is a good thing. We need each in order to have a really great relationship, and they need to be balanced. Even more important is the ability to *combine the two at the same time.* This is the ultimate challenge for those wanting a truly great relationship—how do I remain "me" while having a deep, intimate relationship with "you"?

In chapter 6, we described dating as a process that includes hurting and being hurt, and in chapter 7, we examined the premise that we match up with people whose "emotional cups" are roughly equal to ours. If your cup is one-quarter full of emotional fuel, we'll guarantee that the person you match up with will also be one-quarter full. And that's where the title of the present chapter comes in. To be "old enough to date" means that you are emotionally full enough to risk the dating process.

It also means that you let go of the *pseudo-grown-up* notions that so many of us carry into our twenties, thirties and even our forties. On some psychological tests, there is a scale to measure Socially Desirable Responses, because some people just say what they *think* are the psychologically healthy things to say. Of course, it is a sign of defensiveness to answer this way. This is the kind of stuff that often fits into the category of Foreclosed Identity described in Appendix A—I'm not fully grown up, but I think that a grown-up would answer this way, so I'll fake it by answering what I think is the grown-up way, so that I look like a grown-up! For example, when referring to the fact that normal adults *do* fight about little things, we wrote in chapter 6 that if you say you shouldn't be fighting about little things anymore because you and your partner are adults, then "perhaps you aren't a grown-up yet because these *are* the things that grown-ups fight about."

Over the years, we have found the material we present here and in Appendix A to be by far the most helpful to our clients. Knowing the steps involved in growing up—in filling up the cup—gives each one of us a road map that becomes priceless when, as adults, we discover that we have lost our way. The science of "how we become old enough to date" is invaluable.

Filling the Cup: Erikson's First Five Stages Leading Up to Adult Intimacy

We now return to the emotional cups, which are reproduced in Figure 9.1. We have found it helpful to remind people that each of us works to fill his cup until the day he dies, and then it is still not quite full. In other words, growth and development never end, which is why healthy people do not get bored with their lives for very long. As

Elisabeth Kübler-Ross[14] demonstrated so elegantly in her work with the terminally ill, it is *never too late* to do some "cup-filling." Even if you *believe* that you're too old to fill the cup—that you are too set in your ways to grow up—it isn't true, it's just the *belief* that's keeping you stuck. We've worked with people in their eighties who made remarkable strides in growing up, after being stagnant for decades.

Figure 9.1

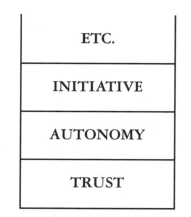

Your "emotional cup" is filled in as you progress
through Erikson's life stages.

There are a number of conceptual frameworks and theories that can each be useful in describing what goes into the cup. We encourage therapists to find a theory of human development that they can work with, and then use it as a foundation—as the infrastructure, so to speak—of the clinical work that they do. The theory that we have found most personally useful is that of Erik Erikson.[15] Despite some of the focused criticisms that have been leveled at certain specifics of his model in the past thirty years, we find that as an overall framework, it is very useful and resilient. So, if you can visualize your inner "self" for a moment as being held within the container in Figure 9.1, we will begin with a brief, informal description of what has to be inside of it for any of us to form a lasting and rewarding romantic bond with another person. If you are not intimately familiar with these stages, we strongly urge you to study the extended descriptions of how each stage is filled in Appendix A.

1. *Trust:* You must have enough *trust* in yourself and in life itself that no matter what happens in the dating process and beyond, you will endure—you'll be okay.

2. *Autonomy:* You must be enough of a *separate individual* (i.e., you must be *individuated* or *differentiated* enough, as Murray Bowen[16] would call it) to be able to risk giving up the relationship rather than lose your identity while in it. This will make it much less likely that the relationship will ever end. If you trust enough and you are separate enough, you will be able to tolerate being apart from your beloved without punishing him or her before and/or during and/or after his or her return from a five-day business trip.

3. *Initiative:* If you have the ability to *make things happen*— i.e., the ability to initiate action—without feeling unduly guilty all the time, then you will be able to express your needs and wants in the relationship, and you will be able to make decisions for yourself that will bring fresh air and healthy change into the relationship. In other words, you will *seldom get stuck* in your life.

4. *Competence:* If you have developed, and continue to

develop, your *competencies*—political, social, emotional, academic, or artistic skills, to name a few—in other words, if you are a *competent person* (keeping in mind that we all have strengths and limitations), then you will be able to take care of yourself even if you are single (pay your bills, do worthwhile work, do your laundry, ask for help when you need it, have self-esteem that is based on something solid, have friends who allow emotional warmth and connection), which will also make it more likely that the relationship will endure.

5. *Identity:* If you have a solid *identity*—if you know who you are, if you *live by convictions* that have been *earned through questioning and struggle*—then you will be able to fully exist inside of a relationship without losing your *self* in the process.

These five "cup-fillers" will get your cup a little more than halfway full, depending upon how you want to play with the metaphor. In today's American culture with our extended education and the dependency on family that goes with it, these first five are usually "filled in" somewhere between the ages of twenty-one and thirty-two. In the lists below, you can see examples of what it looks like if you have filled in each stage fairly well.

Trust vs. Mistrust: Birth to Eighteen Months

- I know the world has dangers in it, but in general, I feel okay, safe.
- There are people with whom I can share "the real me."
- I do not make a crisis out of every setback that happens to me.
- During times of crisis, I know whom I can lean on for support.
- I believe that despite all our flaws, human beings basically mean well.
- I would be devastated if my spouse died, but I know I would get through it.

Autonomy vs. Shame and Doubt: Eighteen Months to Three Years

- I have a very different opinion about the death penalty than my friends do.
- I needed to get away by myself for a few days, so I drove up to the lake and had a very relaxing three-day weekend.
- It is okay with me that my husband voted for a different Senate candidate in the last election. We don't have to be the same on everything.
- My feelings about this are okay, even though they're different than yours.
- I do not panic or rage when my partner is out of town on a business or other trip.

Initiative vs. Guilt: Three to Six Years

- I decided I'd just go down there and apply for that job. Who knows? Maybe I'm more marketable after raising four kids than I thought!

- C'mon, get dressed up! We're going out. I've made dinner reservations for 7:30. It's a surprise!

- I finally signed up for that race I've been wanting to do for so many years. I never thought I could do it! Now I am so excited!

- I sent a letter to everyone in our office building regarding that entrance door being inadvertently locked while our clients are still coming in for appointments at night.

- When I get stuck, I usually find a way out pretty quickly. I always have choices.

Industry vs. Inferiority: Six to Eighteen+ Years

- I like the fact that I do my job well.

- I want to learn how to put together a five-course Northern Italian meal.

- I feel great! I finally figured out how to use this new software.

- I think I need to take this case in for some consultation. I think I'm missing something here.

- I was very pleased with how that presentation went that I gave today.
- I have the skills I need to make it in the world.

Identity vs. Identity Confusion: Roughly Thirteen to Thirty-Two Years

- I changed majors twice, and then took two different university teaching jobs before I realized that American literature was my true passion.
- I am definitely a good tennis player, but when it comes to math, forget it.
- I am an introvert. It took me awhile to embrace that, because everyone else in my family is extroverted. I know what my deepest strengths are, and I also know the challenges of being an introvert.
- It took me a lot of reading, soul-searching, and trying out different religions and even churches, mosques, and synagogues, before I decided where my heart is truly peaceful, spiritually.
- I feel like I know who I am, and that I've earned it through experience.

If you are grounded in trust, can be a separate individual standing alone on her own two feet, can initiate action especially when stuck, have competencies necessary to survive in your particular culture, and have a pretty clear sense of who you are that has emerged from a period of searching and struggle rather than from simply being a "good boy" or a "good girl," then you get to move to the next square on the board—*adult intimacy.*

Intimacy States

Erikson and researchers who followed in his footsteps, like James Marcia, described the four identity states that are presented in detail in Appendix A: Identity Achieved, Moratorium, Foreclosed, and Identity Diffused/Confused. They believed, and later demonstrated, that people were not able to achieve truly intimate relationships until a significant portion of their identity "work" had been done. In fact, Marcia and his colleagues[17] demonstrated a nice parallel between the identity states, above, and the intimacy states, listed here:

Intimate

The person who has achieved this state is seen as being emotionally transparent, as having close personal relationships, as caring for both self and others, as being candid, warm and friendly, as not manipulative in relationships, and as having clear boundaries. In the research findings, people in this group were primarily those who were Identity Achieved. The process of becoming Intimacy Achieved is similar to successful passage through the five earlier stages. People need to "try on different hats" in their relationships, just like they needed to do with regard to their identities. We need to date. Perhaps we need to experience what it feels like to be in love with someone who is just like us, and then maybe someone who is the opposite of us. Maybe we need to be with someone who is very intellectual like Mom is, and then someone who is very emotional like Sister is.

We believe that the divorce rate is so catastrophically high for young marriages because when we are young, our identity isn't well-formed, and we haven't had much experience with dating.

Pre-Intimate

These people tend to be searching for the right kind of relationships that fit them. They are somewhat unsure of themselves and their choices in friendships and lover-type relationships. They tend to have more casual relationships without having established the two or so deeper ones common to the Intimacy Achieved group. This group parallels the Identity-in-Moratorium group. At the same time, people in this group are clearly moving toward the goal of more mature intimacy, and they are developing the integrity, as well as the personal experience required to sustain lasting relationships. This is the exploratory phase that is so essential to finding our place in the world.

Stereotyped Intimacy

People who fit this description parallel the Foreclosed Identity group. They seem to "have it all together" but actually self-disclose very little in intimate situations. On the surface they have deep and enduring intimacy, but one or two levels down, it isn't really deep and enduring at all—rather, it is based on stereotyped roles such as "hus-band," "wife," "boss" and so forth. People in this group were originally described as "playing out the American Dream," and while they appeared to have great friends, on the inside they were shown to be more empty than fulfilled and intimate.

As with Identity Foreclosure, Stereotyped Intimacy means that you will be highly anxious even if you appear calm and collected on the outside, and you will be authoritarian in your relationships even if you espouse a more flexible, toler-ant approach to life. Relationships in the shallows tend to be rigid, black-and-white and all-or-nothing, which makes them pretty painful in the long run. Life is not always pre-dictable, and it is even less controllable. The most uncon-trollable part of life is other people. When other people behave in ways that make us uncomfortable, our anxiety increases and causes us to make any number of "dysfunc-tional" adaptations.

The older a person is, the harder it is to leave this state and try to achieve adult intimacy because of the life conse-quences that accumulate, such as children and financial commitments. And, the older a person becomes, the more uncomfortable life becomes, which puts someone in a very tight bind. There is a world of difference between acting "as if" I know who I am, and acting in a certain way because I know who I am. Someone with a relatively full cup will pick up the difference right away. Someone who is Foreclosed or Stereotyped won't see it at all.

Isolated

People who fit in this category tend to be very isolated and almost devoid of any form of intimacy in their lives. They may be actual hermits, or they may live like hermits even though they may work with others during the day. They avoid relationships and are very uncomfortable when others make attempts to make connections with them.

If you have done the things necessary to find a clear identity, and then you have taken the interpersonal risks to learn how to share yourself with others *appropriately,* given the situation, while still maintaining that identity, then you will look something like this:

Intimacy vs. Isolation: Twenty-Three to Forty-Two Years

- Even though I am a bit shy, when I am in a close relationship, I am comfortable sharing the real me with others.

- I have truly good emotional support in my life, not just "a lot of friends" who don't really know me, or such poor boundaries that I believe everyone is "my best friend."

- I can care about others without losing myself in the process.

- I tend to treat peers, people in positions of authority and people who may work under me with the same respect and courtesy—I am neither intimidated by those above me, nor am I rude and condescending to those who have less power than I do.

- I have pretty good social intelligence—I am aware of my impact on others, and have a pretty good sense of how they view me.

Just as our identities can change in various smaller ways across the life span, so, too, can our capacity for intimacy. But our core identity and our core ability to have a close and enduring relationship without losing ourselves in the process are things that do not go away once we acquire them. And neither one of them is acquired without considerable risk, effort and consequence. Many people who come in for relationship therapy are actually coming in for help in growing up. It is not very common for someone to just have "communication problems" and nothing more. As people gradually take responsibility for their own maturity, and then for their own participation in their relationships, the positive changes come.

Being Old Enough to Date

Nobody gets all of this cup-filling done prior to dating. People typically start dating in junior high school nowadays, and you certainly won't have your identity all cleared up by then. In truth, dating and even marriage are part of the identity formation process. But when people come in for help with their relationships, it is crucial for them to begin to look at their own shortages, and to begin to see how those shortages prevent them from having great relationships. If I can look myself in the mirror and say, "You aren't old enough to date!" I can start a process of growing up that will eventually make possible a really great relationship.

In this next section, we will offer some of the symptoms of not being "old enough to date." As you read them, remember that if a journey of a thousand miles begins with the first step, then realizing your own limitations *is* that first step.

I Can't Live Without You

Country music aficionados know this theme well. "My baby's left me, and I've been drunk for days. I'm about to do myself in, but my dog has to go out, so I'm saved—for another day." The biggest tragedy that happens in relationships between people who haven't grown up yet is the stark terror at even the thought of being apart. This terror is the central reason that people beat each other up, abuse each other verbally, cheat on each other, drink and smoke themselves to death, and so much more.

In terms of the cups, it goes right down to the depths of trust. Our uneducated guts tell us that our trust issues will all be solved if only we can make this relationship work. Reality says something different. The only way to repair this problem is to develop some ongoing, intimate, *nonsexual* relationships that endure over a fairly long period of time. In other words, we need to create a "family" of loving humans with whom we can build a history by the day-to-day process of interacting with them. This is the major reason that we have run the same men's and women's therapy groups for nearly two decades. It's a great way to fill in this part of the cup.

Whether it's through a therapy group or by gradually developing nonsexual, intimate relationships in some other way, this trap is not going to go away until you find a way to meet your emotional dependency needs without trying to engulf or absorb another individual human being. It means struggling with relationships, losing them, licking your wounds and then trying again, with the overriding knowledge that you can't use any one relationship to fill your cup, because that would destroy the relationship.

Me, Me, Me

Martin Buber wrote of the "I" and the "Thou" in relationships.[18] The "Me, Me, Me" stance precludes the "Thou" part of his formulation. Psychoanalysts have embraced the notion of narcissism since the beginning, and the rest of us know that it is one of the features of being human that is the most vexing, perplexing and intriguing of all. We all want to be special. We all want recognition from others. We all want our moment in the sun.

But if we were spoiled or made to feel like we were more special than anyone else in the family, or we were hurt and made to feel like we were less special than anyone else in the family, then we may enter adulthood feeling like we are *entitled* to things to which no one is entitled. No one is entitled to a great relationship. No one is entitled to be happy. It's the *right* to life, liberty and the *pursuit* of happiness—not the *right* to be happy. *Nobody* has the right to be happy. We have to earn it. Comedian Steven Wright said it best: "You can't have everything. Where would you put it?"

The path to earning peace and wholeness is often in conflict with our narcissism, because the only way to be truly
happy is to embrace our disappointments and become
enriched by them. If I am constantly disappointed unless I
get my own way, my relationships will be tense, strained
and exploitive on my part. Others either won't like it, or
they'll tolerate it because they have the complementary
problem, listed next.

People who have particularly strong struggles with this
issue do well when they examine their underlying belief systems about the world. For example, it is good to ask yourself the following questions:

1. What would happen if I just sat back for an hour and
   let someone else take center stage?

2. If I did that, what might I notice that I ordinarily tend
   to miss? With whom might I connect in ways I nor-
   mally wouldn't have connected?

3. If I'm not always the center of things, will I still get
   "enough"?

4. How am I keeping others away from me by doing this?
   Would my underlying fear of never getting enough
   actually *lessen* if I took an interest in others' needs and
   wants as well as my own?

The exaggerated autonomy in the Me, Me, Me syndrome
isn't really autonomy at all. It stems from a deep lack of
trust. Repairing and deepening our relationships with
others, and learning to have empathy toward and understanding of others, are the keys to repairing this problem.

Whatever You'd Like, Dear

We believe that as with all coping strategies and defenses, people who use this one are unaware of how manipulative it can be. It is not "nice" to be so agreeable all the time that you disappear, leaving no one with the privilege of getting to know the real you. It certainly makes sense as a child's coping strategy if he or she is growing up in a family with some fairly big shortages. After all, if the family rule is to be quiet, do your chores, don't question authority figures, stay out of the way when you aren't needed and don't ask for too much, then it makes sense that I might develop the "Whatever You'd Like, Dear" approach.

What is my payoff for being so "nice," so "agreeable" and so accommodating *all the time?* I get to be the good guy. I get to stay out of the line of fire. I don't have to stick my neck out and leave myself open to whatever—to criticism, rejection, conflict, struggle, anger or to strife between us. It's a "safe" strategy, so to speak, as long as you notice the quotes we put around the word "safe." It isn't really safe at all. It is lonely, scary, shaming, hurtful and can make us physically ill.

But grown-ups don't act this way. Yielding too much is just as bad as demanding your way all the time, because it prevents intimacy. Often, problems in this arena can be traced back to the Initiative vs. Guilt step in Erikson's model. Taking the initiative doesn't just mean doing dramatic things like running for president of the United States. It means asserting yourself in thousands of little ways. Whenever you assert yourself, there is the potential for someone else to be angry or disappointed. Learning to allow others to feel angry and disappointed when it is necessary is part of overcoming this difficulty. When you learn that to provide resistance on occasion is the only way you can truly be *in* a relationship, rather than *out* of it all the time, you will have one more stone in place on the path toward having a really great relationship.

So, You Think You Can Hurt *Me*?

Being strong is an asset unless you're too strong. Then, it is being invulnerable. Being invulnerable means being impenetrable. It means I can never open up and let you in. It means I won't ever show my hurt, shame, fear, sadness or loneliness. I will be strong, perhaps aggressive. I will be tough. I can take it, I tell you. I am a rock. I am an island. I have been hurt many times before, starting in childhood, when my father died, or perhaps when my mother criticized me all the time. Maybe I made a silent vow that I would never let anyone hurt me again. And when I got hurt in my first love relationship, it hurt so badly that I didn't get into another one for several years.

Now, as I try to have a marriage with you, I am finding that discomfort and struggle are part of every relationship. But I have my vow. So if you think you can hurt *me,* you've got another "think" coming! I am a rock. I am an island. But I will be alone again sooner than I know, because while never getting hurt may seem like a strong and admirable goal, it is actually a sign that I'm not old enough to date. When I decide that I can open up enough to be hurt, while remaining strong and self-reliant enough to protect myself and deepen in my relationship with you, then I will be on the road to a great relationship.

I'm Too Fragile

Some people are too strong. Others are too fragile. If you fall into this category, then you may find yourself feeling like everyone you date ends up being so mean and insensitive that there is no hope of ever having a great relationship. The only answer appears to be to remain alone and celibate for the rest of your life.

If you are currently *in* a long-term relationship, then you may actually have a great deal of power, whether you are aware of it or not, that derives from the way you express your excessive fragility. You may cry at the drop of a hat. You may recoil from any assertiveness or expressiveness on the part of your mate. You may complain about his or her toughness and rambunctiousness, saying that you can't feel "romantic" or "safe" unless he or she becomes much more peaceful and gentle and kind. You will probably compare yourself to other men or women who are in relationships with perpetrator types who are truly insensitive and mean, but the comparison will be a misguided one. If this is the way you express your lack of being grown-up, then you have the equal but opposite task of the person who "won't ever be hurt again." You need to hang onto *part* of that vulnerability, but temper it with some tough realism as well as some emotional integrity. And remember—nobody can do our growing up for us. You can manipulate all sorts of people into rescuing and coddling you, but if you want a truly great relationship, you'll have to rescue yourself.

You'll Get *Yours*!

Revenge has no place in a good relationship, although *feelings of revenge* belong right in there with the rest of them! So, you think you just hurt *me?* Well, let me tell you something. When I get done with *you,* you'll wish you'd never met me. I am the "master of getting even"!

Doing something constructive with the desire to get revenge is the cornerstone of being a grown-up. Being able to accept and digest the hurts, misunderstandings and disappointments in our relationships without retaliating requires awesome depth and self-mastery. And being able to discern the difference between retaliation and healthy self-protection requires an extraordinary level of wisdom and emotional sophistication.

Human beings are creatures of habit and routine. If I have an annoying habit that you have asked me to alter, the fact that it is a habit means that it may never become altered to your satisfaction. Like a horse with a burr under the saddle, the accumulated distress builds up until one day we lash out with a verbal and physical storm we didn't know existed inside of us. In many cases, it's even harder to reign in the desire to retaliate when the harm is deeper and more painful. Human beings hurt each other for all kinds of defensible reasons. Your spouse has an affair because he's lonely and empty and sad, then he lies about it because he doesn't want to hurt you!

Doing something constructive with the hurt and betrayal, other than to plot revenge, is what will guarantee your "emotional greatness" later on. It isn't so much about "turning the other cheek" and then letting yourself be hurt again and again. It's about turning the other cheek as you begin to protect yourself in the future, and then converting all of that pain-generated energy into something of awesome power and beauty. The story of Myrtle Faye Rumph of South Central L.A., in chapter 13, makes this perfectly clear.

10

Be Sexual

In America sex is an obsession;
in other parts of the world it is a fact.

—Marlene Dietrich

Chapter 10 in distinguished psychologist David
Schnarch's groundbreaking book, *Passionate Marriage: Sex,
Love and Intimacy in Emotionally Committed Relationships,*[19] is
entitled *"Fucking, Doing,* and *Being Done:* It Isn't What You
Do, It's the Way You Do It." The comforting fact about his
book is that after reading the first nine chapters, this chapter
title is not the least bit shocking—it expresses love and integrity. One of the reasons that Schnarch is now considered
to be a leading expert in marital sexuality in this country is
that he was courageous enough to finally address the core
issue in sexual growth and development, that:

115

. . . a couple's sexual repertoire grows through conflict rather than compromise. Sexual conflict in marriage is not just inevitable—it's important . . . {because it} . . . makes both people grow up (p. 259).

It is a powerful, hopeful and some would say revolutionary way to conceive of human sexuality, and in his Passionate Marriage™ and Sexual Crucible™ workshops and seminars, Schnarch devotes several days to help people apply its meaning in their lives or clinical practices. Of course, new ideas make people nervous. You can almost hear the stand-up comedians now: "This man's wife has been complaining to everyone about how she's tired of being married to a little boy. The man yells into the kitchen from the beer-and-football room. 'Hey honey! I just saw a guy on TV who said that sex makes you grow up!' He grins and adds, 'So . . . whaddya say?'"

St. Paul psychologists James Maddock and Noel Larson wrote:

. . . sexuality is a fundamental aspect of human existence. It is one of {the} basic dimensions of human experience, and thus of family life. . . .[20]

Sex is passionate, lusty, sensual, firm, wet, soft and powerful. It is enjoyed, appreciated, desired, feared, used and confused. It is an integral part of spirituality and of relationship, and it is a biological fact.

Lust: It's a Good Thing

One biologist conjectured that billions of years ago a one-celled animal was "eating" another one-celled animal and didn't quite "digest" its prey. The result was that part of its prey's genetic material became incorporated into its own genetic material, and perhaps made the predator and its cell lines more resistant to extinction. And so, billions of years later, we have these little cells with little tails all swimming madly to try to fuse their genetic material with another cell. It is our conjecture that the feelings of "sexual hunger" that two people feel for each other may have evolved from this initial "dietary hunger" of one little animal "lusting" for another. After all, *in a passionate sexual encounter, people do feel like devouring each other.*

Lust is a normal, healthy part of a romantic relationship. What would it feel like if your partner never lusted after you? Peter Koestenbaum[21] also wrote about how very important it is for you to be both the *subject* and the *object* in a sexual interaction. To be "subject," you have to be able to express your will in the relationship. This happens when you lust after your partner and want to devour him or her sexually. It happens when you initiate a sexual encounter. It happens when you do things specifically because they bring pleasure to your partner. But mature, grown-up sexuality also requires that we be able to be the "object" in the intimate relationship—that we be able to revel in and luxuriate in our partner's lust for us. It requires that we yield, surrender, submit, let go, go with the flow—you pick the word—and to *receive* fully and spontaneously, without guilt or shame or fear of engulfment, which can only be done if you have an intact and strong self inside of you.

Sex is powerful and passionate, which is probably why it sometimes scares people. But the thought of sexually devouring your partner now and then can be a very good thought. Lust can be a good thing. Our friend, Patricia Love, wrote a book entitled *Hot Monogamy.* She asked people to try to describe their most intimate and passionate sexual experiences with each other. One man wrote this:

> *I can't describe it. There have been moments when I felt my partner and I were in the space of ecstasy. She was right there with me. To be way out there in space and to look in her eyes and see that she's way out there, too. For that split second—and it's not necessarily the moment of orgasm—we're both right there and we're at one with the universe.* [22]

Sex in America: Confusion

Comedian, actor and writer Steve Martin joked:

> *I believe that sex is one of the most beautiful, natural, wholesome things that money can buy.* [23]

In *Couplehood,* comedian Paul Reiser wrote:

> *You know what ruins sex for a lot of guys? The letters to* Penthouse *magazine. Have you ever read them? Me neither, but a friend of mine did and he told me. . . .* [24]

The messages inside of these quotes capture some of the confusion about sexuality in America. In many ways, the

United States is the most violent of the industrialized nations—especially in the areas of sexual violence, rape and incest. People get confused by this. But is it, or could it be, our *fear* of each other that causes so much of the violence and sexual "dysfunction"?

As human beings, we long for emotional relationships with others, but relationships bring with them a degree of risk—I could get rejected and hurt. In attempting to avoid the pain of rejection, some people become too lonely and disconnected, and will then use sex as a "quick fix" and "instant intimacy" rather than engaging in risk and the possibility of building solid, enduring emotional relationships. When sex is used as "instant intimacy" without emotional connection, it gets distorted, and pretty soon inappropriate physical sexual acting-out replaces the sexual intimacy of a loving relationship. Then, before long, I can get mad at you for "cutting me off." Then I can become more violent in my demands to sexually connect and act out, all because deep down inside I am starved for relationship with other human beings.

The Madonna/Whore and the Brady Bunch/ Indiana Jones Dilemma

Here's a common dilemma. It's called the Madonna/ Whore Dilemma. For how many decades has this been a theme in books and magazines? A man wants the woman in his life to be the saintly Mother of His Children and All-Around Pillar of Civic Rectitude, but he eventually becomes unhappy and angry because he also wants her to

Fuck with Reckless Abandon Like in Those Letters to *Penthouse* magazine. And the dilemma cuts both ways. A woman wants her husband to be The Great Provider and Father to Their Children but grows discontented and starts to have the wandering eye because she yearns for a man who is dashing and dangerous, and suave and debonair, like some combination of Fred Astaire and Indiana Jones.

One way out of binds like these is to use the word "and." But this introduces another piece of the puzzle to consider— the role of fantasy. Fantasies can be very important road maps to something we want or need. When someone is uncomfortable but hasn't found the healthy way to be comfortable, he may *fantasize first* as a way to *begin* solving the puzzle. If he then looks at his fantasy and assumes that it is absolute reality and the *literal* solution, he will be wrong part of the time. For example, if I'm lost in the desert and am nearly delirious from dehydration, I might actually reach for *any* liquid that I come across because the unconscious part of my mind is almost completely running the show at that point. In the same way, if I'm a late-stage alcoholic and I can't find whiskey, I might drink rubbing alcohol.

In desperation, humans often go after something that is a *symbol* or a *representation* of the real thing, believing, in our pain, that it *is* the real thing. The key is that this is not all wrong—we just need to insert one more step. Suppose you are dehydrated in the desert and you stumble across a spring filled with what looks like cold, clear, clean water, but a sign recently posted there says "POISON! DO NOT DRINK!" and right beneath it, on the same sign, it says "INTERSTATE HIGHWAY 10 ONE-QUARTER MILE

AHEAD!" You'd know what to do. You're on the right track. You just need to go a little farther before you get the real thing.

When it comes to the Madonna/Whore or Brady Bunch/Indiana Jones Dilemmas, you need to keep the same thing in mind. What you fantasize may not be what you really want. In Christian theology, the Virgin Mary is one-of-a-kind—she had the only virgin birth that ever did or ever will exist. Does a man really want *her?* That seems sort of sacrilegious. But if he wants someone *like* her—if she is a symbol or a sign pointing toward something else—then what might that be? We posed this question to a man who was caught in this bind and he said, "I want a woman who is trustworthy. Who has character. Who won't cheat on me and hurt me like I've been hurt before."

"Ah," we said. "Now you're onto something."

But he was still in the bind. He said that his wife *was* trustworthy and faithful, but that she didn't like sex. He said he was filled with anxiety, guilt and anger from the moral crisis spawned by his *fantasies* of visiting prostitutes and having sex with reckless abandon. Looking puzzled, we pursued it by saying, "So, feeling hollow, empty and lonely is what you are yearning for in sex?"

"What do you mean by *that?*" he asked.

"Well, consider the level of emotional connection in your fantasy. If 90 percent of prostitutes were sexually abused as children, and prostitution is the ultimate reenactment of hollow, exploitive sex by a powerful adult perpetrated on an innocent child, can this kind of sex produce feelings of intimacy, closeness and wholeness?"

He was silent, seeming to waver between confusion and insight.

The question then becomes: What is the fantasy of having reckless, spontaneous sex with a prostitute a *sign* or a *symbol* of? It's a sign that points not to hollow, empty sex, but to the *deep, warm, intimate, luxurious, spiritual, holy, connected experience of wild, passionate, unfettered, animal sexuality between two people who love, cherish, respect and adore one another.* Sometimes people take their fantasies so literally that they don't get anything useful from them. Some people may actually go out and start having sex with prostitutes in these circumstances! But wouldn't that be like drinking the poison water in the desert? The fantasy is only useful if it causes him to deal directly with his sexual conflict in his real-life relationship. When this happens, it is remarkable how things change.

For Her

I would like to be married to a man who is stable, a good provider and a loving father to our children. And I would like it if, in a way that fits his unique personality, he would be strong enough and grown up enough and separate enough from me to "just take me" now and then. "Taking me" doesn't mean dominating or controlling me. It has absolutely nothing to do with being a bully or a jerk, because if he takes me, it is only because I am woman enough to want the pleasure and intimacy of it, and because I won't lose my identity in the process. It means that he is so taken with me and with his own passion that he gets completely absorbed in himself, me and the moment. He kisses me gently, with his strength, and his strength is rooted deeply, so I can bump against him and not push him over. I know where I am, I know who I am and I know who I love.

For Him

I'd like to be married to a woman who is trustworthy, respectful, open and a loving mother to our children. And I would like it if, in a way that fits her unique personality, she would stand strong in her confidence and hold her ground. I would like her to "just take me" every once in awhile. "Taking me" doesn't mean some kind of empty exploitation of me, nor does it mean a hollow act in which she does something she doesn't really want to do. She can be comfortable and confident in her desire for me. It means that she is so taken with me and with her own passion that she gets completely absorbed in herself, me and the moment. She kisses me gently and passionately. I want someone whose strength is rooted deeply so that I can bump up against her without pushing her over. I know where I am, I know who I am and I know who I love.

Chocolat

The film *Chocolat* was a straightforward portrait of the double-bind that traps many Americans. It shows the depth, purity and integrity of responsible, loving and innocent lust. It shows how the "Powers That Be" can let their own human pain turn from an opportunity for spirituality into an evil engine for the destruction of the human spirit.

It shows the power of the redemption that can only come after a terribly painful battle with what turns out to be the good and gentle forces of life. The film exemplifies the simple paradoxes that exist in everyday life—the supposedly "bad" woman who is the most compassionate of the bunch and the supposedly "holy" town leader who wreaks destruction on innocent people because of his denial and leaves "the rest of us" struggling with what is truly good as opposed to "what looks good."

Lucky in Love

Catherine Johnson[25] wrote that, "A large number of happy marriages, perhaps the majority, are founded on a deeply sexual love. Sexual connection permeates—frequently almost unnoticed—the friendship and working partnership that develop as time wears on." Johnson's book is out of print but is available on used book Web sites like Bibliofind. It is one of the finest studies of marriage we have ever seen, and we would love to see it come back into print.

In it, she conducted in-depth interviews with one hundred couples married seven years or more. Fifty-six of the couples were what she described as "thriving" and "very happily married." Her observations and insights, and the way the book is written, paint sparklingly clear pictures of great relationships with just enough poetic language to be significantly more accurate than had she simply stuck to the science of it all. And when it came to looking at the role of sex in people's lives, she was very forthright in saying that while the old "saws" of companionship and nonsexual intimacy are indeed key features of excellent marriages, it was obvious when she was finished with her interviews *that sex certainly does not die out* seven to ten years into the relationship.

David Schnarch[26] also makes it perfectly clear that a vibrant, passionate sex life is a very normal and *permanent* part of what he calls a *differentiated* relationship. When we hear two people say that their sex life is nonexistent, our ears perk up and we listen carefully, because invariably it is a sign that there are some exciting improvements that they will be able to make in their relationship, when the time is right. And in most cases, there is no time like the present.

What Schnarch unequivocally emphasizes and Johnson's lovely descriptions and quotes from interviewees imply is that sexuality isn't about technique. It has very little to do with the Masters and Johnson stuff that so many of us learned in graduate school. It has much more to do with the chemistry that was there from the beginning coupled with the ongoing and increasing differentiation of both people.[27] Schnarch does an excellent job of ensuring that his readers don't confuse "differentiation" with "being distant, detached and aloof." To the contrary, as it is with the "levels of relationship" that we discussed and demonstrated in chapter 7, the deeper you go into a relationship, the closer you become, but it is only safe to go that deeply when you have the inner-structure—the ego strength or internal boundaries around the "self"—to protect yourself and keep yourself intact *without having to exit the relationship all the time.* Allowing ourselves to acknowledge and focus our anger *constructively* is what makes this possible. The deeper we become related, the more likely we will be to step on one another's toes now and then. My ability to firmly say "Ouch!" when you step on my toe ensures that you won't keep doing it and eventually crush my toe in the process.

Sexuality and Spirituality

About twenty-five years ago, we were doing a series of public workshops on various health topics in a small Midwestern community of twenty-six thousand. When we came to the one on sexuality, we decided to emphasize how important it was for people to relax and enjoy their love-making, in the moment, rather than constantly evaluating how well they were doing. "Performance anxiety" was seen as a major sexual problem for people. We wanted to help them relax and stop self-observing so much, when what they were doing was supposed to be spontaneous and pas-sionate. So we thought we would lighten up the title by calling the workshop, *Sex: If God Had Wanted Us to Be Perfect, He Would Have Made Us That Way.*

Despite a clear explanation of the workshop topics in large, bold bullets right beneath the title, the phone rang off the hook for most of two days, the primary complaint being that some people thought we were advocating extra-marital affairs. The topic of "sex" can have that effect.

Sexuality and spirituality *are* related, despite the artificial attempts to separate them over the centuries in the service of "mind-body dualism." To help clarify the relationship between the two, we wrote the following in 1991:

Spirituality and Sexuality

For healthy people, sex is sometimes serious, sometimes fun, sometimes gentle, sometimes wildly passionate and freeing, sometimes inventive, sometimes playful, and sometimes just plain old comfortable. And sometimes, for one brief eternal moment, a sexual experience between two people who actually love each other produces a spiritual fusion of selves that would be terrifying were the couple not healthy and separate at the same time that they became "lost" in each other. Almost anyone can experience the fusion and "apparent ecstasy" of such encounters, but it is the dynamic tension between loss of self and keeping of self that lets two people experience the spiritual ecstasy of their sexuality. When you have felt particularly whole inside of yourself, and when you have been able to cherish the dignity and fragileness of your partner while cherishing your own dignity and fragileness, and then the two of you have been able to merge your "selves" without losing your identity, then you have had a uniquely spiritual experience.

Spirituality and Good Works

Now, let's look at someone like Mother Teresa. She's a young nun riding on a train. She gets this idea that she's supposed to go to Calcutta and not just help the poor, but live with the poor. She's supposed to be poor. She's supposed to fuse with the poor but stay separate enough to do some good and not burn out or lose her sanity in the process. She's supposed to fight but be gentle, be strong but compassionate, be innocent but politically astute, work hard but not work herself to death, have joy amidst incredible sorrow, maintain her privacy but be with thousands, do it miraculously but remain humble, and be vulnerable without being needy. In other words, she's supposed to cherish the fragileness and dignity and power of the suffering souls in the gutters and alleys of Calcutta while cherishing her own fragileness and dignity and power at the same time. That's spirituality in its simplest form—actions, thoughts and feelings.[28]

Healthy, spiritual people who love each other find that their sexual life, rather than getting boring over the years, is an important part of their communication and of their celebration of their relationship. Sexual intercourse and orgasm are a beautiful physical metaphor for life and death itself, as Koestenbaum pointed out. We come together, join physically and emotionally, share a physical and emotional ecstasy unparalleled in our sensory experience, and then we must separate again. We don't want to separate, but we must, and so we do. During a healthy sexual experience, we become highly vulnerable and open to another human being, to ourselves, and to the universe. People who have an open stance toward life in general, and who can be vulnerable when it is safe, do not have sexual dysfunctions that we know of, except in the case of physical problems. Likewise, people who are open and vulnerable in their lives do not have a paralyzing fear of death.

People who are sexually repressed may be afraid of their feelings in general, not just their sexual ones. This explains the accompanying fear of the risks involved in nonsexual intimacy. Being unable to experience feelings clearly, and being fearful of intimacy, makes the even more mature and abstract task of being spiritual very difficult for many people. Having a spiritual experience requires that we let go of our control and then surrender to what is more powerful than we are. We open ourselves up to creation and become vulnerable and powerful all at the same time. We feel at one with creation. We have a tearful, joyous awe and wonder about the unknowable in the universe. We are afraid and unafraid in the same breath, and we are infinitely humbled by the experience.

Do you see the connection between spirituality and sexuality? What we just wrote could be used to describe a spiritual experience that you had while in church, that you had while looking up at the star-filled night sky, that you had while in a caring conversation with a friend, or that you had while having sexual intercourse with your partner.

Watch a truly romantic love scene in a film that is filled with understated passion and tasteful erotic energy, and you will see sexuality that is beautiful, powerful and spiritual. Notice what you feel as you watch. Notice what a risk it is for two adults of equal power to approach each other sexually. Healthy sexuality between two adults of equal power is a wonderful, holy celebration of life itself, regardless of one's religious orientation.

Pulling or Pushing or Fitting or Putting It All Together

We use sex to sell everything from water pumps for our automobiles to romantic tropical cruises, and then before we have enough time to say "orgasm," we turn around and someone is telling us that sex is the root of all evil. We package it, promote it, push it, exploit it and glorify it; and then we condemn it, vilify it, demonize it, repress it and denounce it from the highest mountain. We swing from one extreme to the other, lusting for our spouses one minute and feeling guilty the next. No wonder many of us are confused. For the benefit of those who still question the moral goodness of sexuality, we also wrote the following in 1991:

> *A 1991 cover story in* U.S. News & World Report *was entitled "Sex and Religion: Churches, the Bible and Furor over Modern Sexuality." We are obviously still confused and upset by sex. {And yet}, in* Embodiment, *theologian James Nelson noted that, "To the Hebrews sexuality was a good gift from God." Later denial of the goodness of the body came in part from "Persian beliefs which correlated salvation with sexual restriction."*[29]

In other words, sex is a good thing, even if some good people believe it is not so good.

"Sensible" Sex

You'll never make sense out of sex unless, in addition to your lover, you embrace two things:

1. Sex is about the senses;
2. Sex is about intimacy.

In *Reason and Emotion,* British philosopher John MacMurray zeroed in on just how important the world of our senses is. If ever there were an argument disputing the artificial split between our bodies and our minds, this is it.

The senses are the gateways of our awareness. They are the avenues along which we move into contact with the world around us. Without this sensuous awareness of the world, no consciousness and no knowledge of any kind is possible, for human beings at least. Even our knowledge of God is only possible through the awareness of the world which our senses provide.[30]

To be a good lover, a person must learn to see, hear, smell, taste and touch. She must learn to notice what she finds pleasurable and what she doesn't find pleasurable. She must learn to communicate with her partner about her sensuality and her sexual likes and dislikes. If something drives your husband wild, but he doesn't tell you what it is, how will you ever know? Do you know what he wants and likes? If something drives your wife wild, but she never tells you, how will you ever know? Do you know what she wants and likes?

We are sensory and sensual beings. We have senses so that we can gather information about the world, but also for pleasure. That's what "pleasing to the senses" means. It is not evil to enjoy the sight of fresh flowers in a vase on your kitchen table. It is not evil to enjoy the smell of freshly baked bread. It is not evil to enjoy the cozy patter of rain falling on your roof. Life is a combination of pleasure and discomfort. It should not be all discomfort, and it should not be all pleasure. There needs to be a balance. To enjoy our sensuality is part of the joy of being human. If we weren't supposed to feel pleasure, we wouldn't have it wired into our brains.

Our genital sexuality is simply one part of our much broader sensuality. We certainly experience sex through our senses. But our sensuality is much more than just sexual. People get shut down to the point that they don't appreciate anything that they take in through their senses, and then they wonder why their sexual organs don't work. Retrain your eyes, ears, taste buds, nose and skin to take in the world around you. After that, see how your sex life has improved. But remember, you may have to overcome some unhealthy guilt that tells you that it is bad to be pleased. Just remember the flowers on the table or the freshly baked bread, and that will help melt away the guilt.

As sex is a metaphor for life and death, it is also a reflection of the level of intimacy that we share. If you aren't quite emotionally old enough to date, you may begin to do something different with your sexuality. You may use it to act out your anger and disappointment by withdrawing from your partner, or worse, by comparing your partner to someone from your past. Or you may use it as a distraction to avoid the conflicts altogether. Some people say that their sex life is "fantastic" but that every other part of their relationship is in a shambles.

Remember, too, that sex is a subset of intimacy. Part of intimacy is intellectual, in which we share our thoughts and beliefs and knowledge. Part of intimacy is behavioral, in which we share things like chores, hobbies and the like. Part of it is social, in which we share ourselves with friends. But the part that confuses many people is that of emotional communication—*sharing feelings. It is absolutely essential for the health of a relationship that both people are able to share feelings, including the ones that aren't so easy to share.* It is a very intimate act to stop in the middle of a busy evening, look your partner in the eyes, and tell her that you are grateful that she is in your life. It is intimate to share with her how embarrassed you felt when you flubbed your presentation at the board meeting that afternoon, or how sad and lonely you feel because you had a falling out with your brother. It is also a very intimate act to tell your partner that his breath is really bad and that you would appreciate it if he would brush his teeth. If this is a constant problem and you tell yourself that it isn't important enough to mention, someday you'll explode and tell him in a very hurtful way. Whenever you share something that reveals your true, inner-self to your partner, it is a gift of intimacy and an act of love.

Now, think about this: If you don't share your day-to-day feelings with each other because it's too risky or difficult, how on Earth will you be able to communicate with each other sexually? You won't. You will have a mediocre sex life at best. And it is very possible that you will secretly resent your partner or feel deep shame about yourself, all because neither of you is willing to be vulnerable with each other as you tell each other what you need sexually.

Healthy couples eventually take the huge intimate risk of becoming emotionally vulnerable to each other so that their hurts and wounds from the past can be healed. But this can only happen if each person maintains his or her separate identity in the process. It is as important to be separate in a relationship as it is to be together. As a couple takes these deeper emotional risks, their sexuality becomes firmly embedded in a much broader context of separateness, dignity, compassion and emotional closeness.

In other words, our sexuality needs to become a humble yet ecstatic part of something bigger—our love for each other.

11

Be Willing to Divorce

The trouble is, if you don't risk anything,
you risk even more.

—Erica Jong

Really great couples are willing to end it all, and so
they never have to.

A woman was grousing around her kitchen, silently
shouting to herself, *I don't know* why *I stay with him! He is
so arrogant!* At that moment, she hated her partner more
than anyone she could imagine, including that politician
she voted against in the last election! She charged back and
forth, flinging dirty dishes into the dishwasher as she tried
to prepare dinner for their toddler. "Damn!" she exploded
aloud. "If it weren't for those damned blue eyes of his, I'd
be out of here in a New York minute!" She paced some
more, as, in the space of a nanosecond, the usual pictures

135

flashed through her mind's eye—push for that promotion at work, then contact an attorney, begin reaching out to friends, find a place to live, then have "the meeting" with him and tell him that it's finally over, then the grief, then tell the kids without putting them in the middle and without burdening them with unnecessary details, then sell the house, set up separate households, go forward with the final court action, finish it up, get some counseling for everyone, grieve some more, start a new life alone, then, someday, start dating again.

If you counted every household in which this happens over the course of a year, we suspect you'd count into the millions. If you think it never happens in yours, we encourage you to ask yourself why. In *All's Fair: Love, War and Running for President*[31] James Carville and Mary Matalin describe the scene the night that William Jefferson Clinton won the 1992 election for president of the United States. It is one of the more delightful true-life descriptions of two very politically different people falling ever more deeply in love with each other as one momentarily, and understandably, finds herself hating the other from the depths of her soul as the other waits for the dust to settle. People who are deeply and passionately in love with each other must by definition have a strong identity. That they *do* have strong identities means that the sparks will fly from time to time.

The Key to Marital Happiness: It's the Teeth

Keys have teeth. The teeth come in infinite combinations, but when you add them all up, no matter how big or small they are, they do one thing and one thing only—they hit the tumblers in the lock in just the right way that they cause the lock to release and open. The key to marital happiness is like that—infinite combinations of teeth that all add up, in the end, to *magic.*

And, *they are teeth.* They aren't some kind of ethereal pabulum. One of the more intractable fantasies that we encounter in couples who come in for help is the one that says, "If we *really* loved each other, we'd never feel this angry at each other." While deeply loving couples feel like ending it now and then because they're alive and sentient, the tragedy for not-so-happy couples is that they were misled into thinking that, "If you love each other, you'll never *think* about ending it." Thank goodness the human brain is more complex and interesting than that. The truth is that while happy couples feel this way from time to time, something magical prevents them from *acting* on it. In fact, this magical something does more than that. *It works with the "ending it" fantasy to create something more wonderful and marvelous than anyone could ever have imagined had they not been so angry!* If you've been searching for the exact key to marital happiness, here is one of the biggest teeth on the key: *If you're too dependent on your partner to ever go to the brink, your relationship is in danger of becoming stagnant and dead, which will push you over the brink.* It's quite the paradox.

We were working with a wonderful couple for some time, and they were making slow, steady progress. We never try to predict whether a couple will make it or not, but we had a pretty strong sense that they could. Then, as sometimes happens, they bumped into what they called "a deal breaker." It was a difference between them that they sadly feared would end their seven-year marriage. He had grown up in a good midwestern farm family where, as Garrison Keillor describes the residents of his mythical Lake Wobegon, "All the women are strong, all the men are good-looking and all the children are above average"—and what's more, he grew up touch-deprived because of the inherent emotional reserve in his family. As you might expect, he married someone who was more reserved than he would have liked. She didn't like public displays of affection, didn't like hand holding and she wasn't as "cuddly" as he wanted. She was more like his family, in other words.

From her vantage point, he was too affectionate and "touchy-feely," which she interpreted as excessive neediness and clinging. She complained of feeling smothered, and the daily flow of energy between them became strained and choppy. They were locked in a battle between the need for physical space and the need for physical affection. They were also locked in what Harriet Lerner[32] called "The Dance of Intimacy." As he tired of the struggle, he'd give up and back away. When he backed away, she'd feel some breathing room and move towards him. As he backed away a tad more, she felt some fear, too, and moved in a little more. Sensing that she was finally giving him what he needed, he moved back in to soak up all that he had longed for these many months. As soon as he did that, she felt smothered and backed away. They were caught in what David Schnarch calls "gridlock."

Sensing the opportunity provided by this exquisite tension, we offered them this as they were walking out of a session with us: "If a person isn't willing to lose his or her marriage, then it may not be worth keeping." Our next appointment was in two weeks. They had done a lot of groundwork. They had stuck with us through the part of therapy in which we push on each one separately to grasp and digest responsibility for their own part in the problem. The ride home was silent as each of them was pulled right up to The Brink by how they interpreted what we had said.

Two weeks later, they came in and sat down, looking different. They looked like grown-ups. They looked strong, resolute and peaceful despite the obvious unease in the room. Something had shifted. Instead of trying to harp at each other, which we don't encourage anyway, he began by saying, "I was really mad at you two for saying that. I rode home in silence saying to myself, *Who do they think they are? They're trying to ruin our marriage! They as much as said we should get divorced!*"

She added, "I was mad at you, too. You two seem to have a good marriage, and it felt like you were telling us, 'We have a good marriage, you don't, and we think you should just get on with it and end it. Don't keep bothering us with your bad marriage.'" She paused for a moment, composed herself respectfully and continued, "And then it dawned on me. This isn't about you and your marriage. You're the therapists. This is about *our* marriage." Her eyes grew misty as she held her head high and looked directly into his eyes, a woman who now took herself seriously. "I realized that there was something *I* needed to change."

We noticed out of the corners of our eyes that he was suppressing his own tears, not because he was afraid she would get mad at what she saw as his excessive sentimentality, but *because he empathized with the importance of her struggle for her.* Voilà! As she took the risk to step into adulthood in a way she thought impossible, he did the same. Her struggle had nothing to do with his, and his had nothing to do with hers. In other words, as they stood on the edge of the cliff together, they both took a frightening, flying leap into adulthood, and the winner was their marriage.

Going to the Brink/ Putting Your Foot Down

In a truly great relationship, people go to the brink for any number of reasons. They may be at odds over whether to have children or not. One may have an unacknowledged problem, like depression or an addiction, that is serious enough for the other to say, "I love you more than anything else in the world. *And,* if you don't get some help for this problem, I will have to move out, or ask you to move out, until you do, because I'm not willing to sit idly by and watch you go under."

You may be thinking, "Well, he doesn't *really* mean it. He just needs to say that to prod her into action. He wouldn't really leave." But you'd be wrong. What separates the men from the boys and the women from the girls in these scenarios is that they *are indeed* willing to not just go to the brink, but to take the leap off the brink into the great unknown. A scared child might *threaten* to leave a painful relationship, but when it comes to actually doing it, he won't. In some cases, his bluff works and she gets the help she needs. In many more, she senses his underlying weakness and exaggerated dependency and simply stonewalls him.

There are some rather stunning examples of going to the brink, too. Many of us know of a couple who divorced, lived apart for a number of years, started dating again and then eventually remarried each other. In some cases, these are highly unstable people who are confused and acting out, but in others that we have witnessed closely, it is a case of two people needing to grow more before being able to put together a truly great marriage.

And then there is the issue of needing to put one's foot down every once in awhile. We recall the woman in the Seattle area who went on strike against her family many years ago, eventually landing herself on *The Tonight Show* with Johnny Carson. It's a common problem. Mom does all the cleaning and laundry, cooks all the meals, drives the kids everywhere, entertains her husband's business associates, and is somehow expected to be an alert and fantastic lover to boot. Even in dual-career households, most moms still do the majority of the housework. She must have become so fed up with feeling like nobody cared about her because they refused to help around the house, and she must have felt so used and angry that she finally did the unthinkable—she went on strike.

We use this as an example of how each of us is responsible for the lives that we create, and that if we truly want change to happen, we will make it happen. In other words, the dilemma of unequal participation in household chores is caused in part by men not choosing to participate. But it is also caused by women caving in and fearing going to the brink, which is why there is so much nagging in households like this. So think about this woman for a moment. Consider the courage and determination that it must have taken to do such a thing. Imagine the pressure she must have felt from her husband and children, her neighbors and relatives, and from her kids' school. Imagine how embarrassing it must have been, and how scared and guilty she must have felt. Think about how angry she had to be. "Fed up" means just that.

Our interpretation of "fed up" is "full," "finished," "done," "it's over." If someone is truly "fed up," she isn't going to keep eating. If she kept eating, she'd eventually have to throw up, and that would be a mess. Being fed up means that she is not going to take it anymore, and that she will act accordingly. Nagging doesn't change anything. "Change" changes things. So, going to the brink is about taking the initiative versus being paralyzed by guilt and fear, which we discussed in depth in chapter 9.

Equal Exit Power

David Schnarch correctly notes that the person who wants the relationship the least has the most power. But in a truly great relationship, over the long haul, both people are equally attracted to each other, and they would be equally afraid of losing each other. A man said, "Sure, there are lots of attractive women in the world. But why would I let a little bit of my loneliness ruin our marriage while she's out of town? I couldn't lie to her about something like that because when you try to compartmentalize something that important, it automatically begins to erode the foundations of the marriage. If I couldn't lie about it, then I couldn't do it, because I'd have to tell her, and I couldn't bear to hurt my wife because I love her too much. To top it all off, even if I thought I could compartmentalize it without damaging the relationship, I know two things: (1) She would be just as capable of having an outside relationship as me, and (2) she is just as capable as I am of leaving the relationship if things got awful."

Are you wondering if the last two points above sound a bit too much like the principle of Mutual Assured Destruction that kept a nuclear holocaust in check during the Cold War? Rest assured that *if the only thing holding two people together is the fear of each other's retaliation, then it isn't much of a relationship.* No, perhaps the best way to explain the importance of this principle of Equal Exit Power is to say that without it, the relationship is forever drifting in a kind of limbo of patronization. That is, I *choose* to stay in the relationship, whereas you are *desperate* to stay in the relationship. Put another way, the relationship always has an element of risk in it for you, which keeps your passion high, whereas it is too safe for me, which eventually leads to boredom and stagnation. Put yet another way, you could say that when we have Equal Exit Power, we are both "on" or "on our toes" a smidgen more—we take the relationship less for granted; we feel an acuity to it, a cleaner, more intense perception of the relationship, like the difference between a startling, sharp, bright blue autumn sky on the prairie versus a gray, hazy, muddled day in a big city in the doldrums of winter.

Resistance

Resistance allows us to experience each other and the world around us. This is true in all aspects of the natural world whether in a physical, psychological or spiritual sense. When the wind blows through the Sierra Nevada mountains during a late summer thunderstorm it produces the most magnificent, mysterious, soulful noise you could possibly hear. It is not quite a whoosh, not quite a howl, not quite a roar, not quite a moan, not quite a sigh. It is rather as if the spectacular granite mountains themselves had breathed in all of creation and then released it back out into the universe in one strong, steady exhale followed by another. As the air passes through the pine trees it meets resistance from the tree trunks and branches, but it is the resistance that it encounters as it rushes through the millions of delicate pine needles on the trees that accounts for the exquisite sound. Billions of air molecules made up of protons, neutrons and electrons flowing over, under, around and through millions of pine needles. Air molecules colliding with pine needles and pine needles brushing against each other. Together, they produce the sound of the heavens breathing, for the splendid enjoyment of all who could appreciate such things.

The answer to the age-old question must therefore be, "There is a sound of one hand clapping, but only because of the resistance the hand meets as it brushes against molecules of air." William Shakespeare wrote that all the world's a stage, and each person must play his part; indeed, all of life's dramas are played out on this stage of resistance.

Life requires struggle, and struggle requires resistance.

Couples often come to us with resistance dilemmas, although they don't know that at the time. A woman complains that her partner isn't strong or masculine enough. A man is angry at his partner for walking away every time they get into a fight. He laments, "Why can't you just hang in there and deal with me face-to-face once in awhile?" Or one person ends a relationship with another because the other was too agreeable, too accommodating, too easy. And at the opposite extreme, many relationships are in trouble because they possess too much resistance, leading the couples to say, "All we ever do is dig our heels in, fight and then stubbornly resist each other's overtures for a few days just for good measure, so that it never feels like we're together on much of anything."

On any number of occasions over the years, a man in one of our men's therapy groups finds himself struggling with his passivity and fear of disagreement. Although he is intelligent and understands the value of anger and conflict in keeping relationships alive, he seems unable to act on his insight. Whenever his partner gets angry at him whether she is justified or not, his only response is to yield and agree, or withdraw. Of course the more he does this the more disappointed and rageful she becomes, so that the next time something happens she is even more intimidating, which makes him even more afraid of her, and so they appear caught in an endless, downward spiral of what some would call passive-aggressiveness. But we prefer to call it a dilemma of resistance—one creates too much, the other too little.

We encourage the more dominant partner to temporarily

set aside her anger so that she can get to the vulnerability in the deeper parts of her soul. This is a tremendous risk for her because being in charge has been her edge to keep her from being too hurt. The mere thought of sharing power is frightening. At the same time, we begin to help the more yielding partner learn to appreciate the importance of resistance, and then to start providing it.

In men's groups, it can be a very effective illustration to have the man stand up and face another man, both of them with their arms and hands outstretched, palms forward, touching, so that they can maneuver each other around the room by pushing and yielding. We first have them stand there and simply push and yield with their hands and arms, as if they are getting used to the rudder controls of an airplane. As they get the hang of it, they are unconsciously getting a sense of what cooperative resistance feels like at a deep physical level. Next, we ask the typically passive man to provide no resistance as the other man pushes him around the room, forward, left, right, fast, slow. We stop them and ask the passive man how it feels, and he usually says something like, "It's okay," or "It's not too bad," or "I guess I don't like it, I don't know."

Then we ask the passive man to take charge while his partner yields. He appears uncomfortable at first, being unaccustomed to leading in this way, but soon he gets the hang of it and a smile appears at the edges of his mouth as he discovers how good it feels to have some power in relation to another human being. The other group members find themselves filled with grateful relief because they have been carrying the tension of his passivity and his wife's anger inside of them for as long as he has been in the group. This simple exercise becomes a concrete example for what will eventually happen in his marriage—he and his wife will share the power and thereby match each other's resistances. We cannot help but feel lonely when we are in a relationship with one who does not provide resistance because without resistance we can't tell whether or not anyone is there. The other person becomes invisible.

Some people feel that these ideas of independence and resistance are cold and harsh. Others recognize their truth but feel that they are simply too painful and difficult to attain. Indeed, to accept that we cannot fully possess another human being is frightening at first because it taps into our natural fear of abandonment. But the tension produced as we try to balance fusion and isolation is what keeps our relationships vibrant over the years. It truly is what separates the numb relationships from the dynamic ones.

Despite her love for you, an independent person will want time away from you. She will have a part of herself that is just hers, and the moment that she makes the final leap from this world into the next, she will do it alone. The resistance present in a deep relationship between two solitudes is exciting, delicate, ecstatic, fragile and energizing. To use M. Scott Peck's word, it is called "love." When two people have what we call dependency damage, the resistance between them is either so slight that they are mired in emotional muck most of the time, or so strong that they are trapped in intense conflict most of the time. Our outer logic might suggest that we would feel more alive if we swung between the extremes of infantile fusion and infantile rage.

But our inner logic tells us that when two people let go of resistance extremes and move toward subtlety, the exquisite tension that results can keep people feeling alive and connected with life and each other for decades. Subtle resistance is a crucial part of both the early sexual chemistry between partners, as well as the long-term emotional passion in their relationship.

The concept of resistance is also helpful in trying to separate the dynamics of healthy relationships from those of abusive relationships. In a healthy relationship, the overall resistance of one matches the overall resistance of the other, and it is the alternating, subtle yielding of one to the other that accounts for the understated passion that is ever-present between the two. She moves toward him and exerts her will just as he willingly yields. He moves toward her and exerts his will just as she willingly yields. This dance of exertion and yielding that is shared and desired and accepted by both partners accounts for the beauty and magic of their love. In an abusive relationship, he moves toward her, exerts his will against her protests, feels that her resistance is a threat to his being, gets scared, exerts his will some more, meets resistance, and then flies into a rage with the goal of destroying her resistance altogether, and unwittingly crushes her soul and the soul of the relationship in the process. Infants scream and rage when their fantasies meet resistance. Grown-ups savor the exquisite tension allowed by resistance and thus reap its rewards.

The Risks of Being Too Scared to Go to the Brink

Sufi Master Idries Shah said that he had learned never to pay attention to what people say, but instead to only watch what they do. There is only one true measure of the willingness to go to the brink, and that is to go to the brink and not blink. The film *Thirteen Days* did an outstanding job of portraying the complicated political maneuvering between the White House and the Pentagon as John F. Kennedy and Robert F. Kennedy tried to move the United States away from narrow and shortsighted militaristic policies into the era of global politics. And although JFK did not blink, and so prevailed in removing the Soviet missiles from Cuba, he was not so fortunate in prevailing where his own life was concerned. Such are the very real risks of going to the brink. But the risks of *not* going to the brink are *worse*. We want to close this chapter with three examples of what can be worse.

No One Will Take You Seriously

If you believe that you can never draw a line in the sand for fear of losing the relationship, *then you will disappear.* We hear many people, women especially, complain that they feel invisible in their marriages and their families. A woman says, "We always do what my husband or the kids want to do. I've deferred for so many years on the little decisions in life, like which movie to go to or where to go on vacation, that I feel like I hardly exist at all." Men say it, too. But not quite as often.

Our "wants" are what define us. What we like and don't like *differentiates* us from others. If we aren't differentiated from others, then we must be fused with them, and if we are fused with them, we have disappeared into them, like being absorbed into an amoeba. One day a woman we know was riding in the car on the way to the movie theater with her family—the movie already having been selected—and she calmly said, "I think I'm going to go see *Heartbreakers* instead. It starts ten minutes later and gets out fifteen minutes after your movie does. Where would you like to meet after the show?" Well, by the looks of disbelief on the faces of her family, you would have thought she was the guy in all of those *Friday the 13th* movies! The following weekend, they asked her what *she* wanted to see as they began to negotiate the one they'd all go to.

When people don't take us seriously, it is our responsibility to educate them in a manner that will be effective. If telling them directly works, then by all means, tell them directly. But if it doesn't work, and if the issue is important enough, you may have to go a step or two further. If you have gotten everyone to agree that when you get to the cottage at the beach, everyone will unpack their belongings, stow them away properly, and then pitch in and help make lunch for the crew, then you *expect* that. If everyone piles out of the car, flings their suitcases and duffel bags onto the porch, and then heads to the beach for a swim, it's okay for you to do what you need to do to take care of your things, and then maybe you and your partner could walk into town and have a leisurely lunch at the deli. When everyone barges back into the cottage a few hours later, hungry and wondering where you are, they will find a respectful note saying that you'll be back around dinner time, and to help themselves to whatever they want for lunch.

Nagging

Nagging is a sign of impotence. Not sexual impotence. Simply lack of power. Power is the ability to make things happen. When my interactions with you degrade into constant nagging, then it's a sure sign that I've become powerless in that situation. Nagging pushes people away and does nothing to change the behavior. In fact, in many cases, the more a person nags, the more the other person engages in the offending behaviors. Nagging is also offensive itself, and so it is a very effective way to shut down a relationship. But if it's a sign of powerlessness, then what am I to do?

If I keep complaining that my children won't eat the dinner that is placed before them each night, but I continue to make three different meals so that the children won't whine, then it is my fault that this pattern continues. When I decide that the discomfort of watching them go to bed hungry for one night will be less than the exhaustion and shame that come with making multiple meals each night, then I will stop nagging and *do* something about it. People typically get caught in the circularity of nagging because of the fear of what might happen if they *stop*. If I stop, I either surrender to the misery in which I am trapped, or I face shaking up the system. Each day, it's a choice.

You and the Relationship Will Begin to Wither and Die Inside

When you aren't willing to put your foot down now and then, the sparks begin to die out. The only two types of people who want to be in a relationship with a victim are either another victim or a perpetrator. Healthy people don't like the manipulation and martyrdom that go with the victim role. Adults don't like to be in a relationship without any resistance. It doesn't feel good. It doesn't have any energy in it. It feels stale.

People are afraid of change for a good reason—change is scary. When either one of you puts your foot down about something, by definition you are causing change to happen in other people's lives, because we are interconnected within our family systems. The outcomes of *not* putting your foot down can be scarier still, but because they are farther away in time, they don't *feel* as scary when we're trying to make the decision.

We encourage people to slow down and look into the future when they are trying to extricate themselves from seemingly intractable problems. Sometimes the scariest solutions turn out to be the easiest and most kind for all concerned. Everybody wants to know what the score is from time to time.

12

Know How You Chose Each Other

But ever since the dawn of civilization,
people have not been content to see events
as unconnected and inexplicable. They have craved
an understanding of the underlying order in the
world. Today we still yearn to know why we are here
and where we came from.

—Stephen Hawking
A Brief History of Time

We Can Learn a Lot When Things Go Wrong

The Parent You "Like" the Most May Be Your Biggest Problem

If you are having significant troubles starting or maintaining an adult romantic relationship, and *if* you had some notable (although it could be covert) dysfunction in childhood and *if* you find it easier to feel more positively toward one parent than the other, *then* it is often this parent who is your biggest problem! The more I am bonded with, and feeling protective of, one of my parents, the more I will make the same error (or exact opposite) as him or her, in my intimate relationships.

We put "like" in quotations above because it may be that you:

1. Feel sorry for this parent
2. Are more sympathetic to his plight
3. Feel like she at least tried to show you some care, concern or warmth
4. Took as much, if not more, abuse from your other parent than you did
5. See this parent as helpless, a victim or powerless
6. Were spoiled or babied or otherwise made to feel "special" by this parent
7. Feel more warmly toward her
8. Could at least talk to him about things
9. Etc., etc., etc.

This is one of the most powerful observations that we can

make in the middle or later stages of therapy, and it is one of the most difficult yet most productive awarenesses that anyone can have as they try to mature. The reason it is so important is because the blinder that rests beneath this small fact is actually huge—and its greatest impact is on one's romantic relationships. Here are a couple of examples.

A boy feels sorry for Father because Mother has a nasty disposition and takes it out on him all the time. Father doesn't defend himself, choosing to remain the "nice guy" and to reap those "nice guy" benefits. The son grows up and finds himself choosing and then getting trapped inside of painful, critical, unfaithful or otherwise abusive relationships with women. He will often repeat this pattern for a long time, until he is able to look at his father as realistically as he already looks at his mother. As long as he believes that "all women are manipulative, unfaithful and volatile," those will be the only kinds of women he chooses, and the only kinds of women who choose him.

A girl feels sorry for Mother because Father had obvious multiple affairs, lied about them all, spent all the family money on himself and then turned it all around and blamed mother for "being frigid." The daughter grows up and finds herself getting into relationships where she is lied to, cheated on, betrayed or otherwise hurt, but finds herself getting twisted into knots of confusion as these men justify and rationalize their dishonest behavior. Until she acknowledges and faces what she learned from her mother, she will continue to be in "brain-lock" whenever he tosses his ridiculous explanations her way. As long as she frames her problem as "men are dishonest, cheatin' rats," she'll be trapped, and she'll continue to unconsciously choose unhealthy men. What *healthy* man would ever go out on a second date with an angry woman who believed that all men were "dishonest, cheatin' rats"?

The Affair

You can learn a lot about a system when it malfunctions. So, you can learn a lot about someone by looking at the person with whom he or she has an affair.

"My husband is stiff and straightlaced and responsible," a woman says. "My lover is more 'nontraditional' or 'an artist' or 'more sensitive' or 'more passionate' or much 'kinder and gentler.'" A man says, "Tracy isn't like my wife. My wife is passive, uninterested in sex and way too emotional. I feel like she's almost fragile. My lover is 'a tiger'! She's tough, too. I like that." Very often people will describe their new lover as "not like my spouse at all."

It is true that we pick people who are our emotional equals. It is also true that we often pick people who have a quality that we lack, or that balances a trait of ours that is pushing out toward the extremes. Someone who is just "a little too kind" will typically pick someone who is "just a tad on the unkind side," one who is quiet will tend to pick one who is loud, one who is neat and organized will pick one who isn't. These are the differences that keep the sparks of passion flying but that also try men's and women's souls. This is why it is said that what we adore about each other is also what we hate about each other when we're "in a hatin' kinda mood."

The fascinating part about an affair is that people actually say, "If I could just combine the traits of my spouse and my lover, I'd have the perfect partner!" But take a careful look at Figure 12.1. Pretend that you are the one labeled "Me." You never imagined that you would *ever* be capable of having an affair, but here you are, in the middle of one, shocked and confused and energized all at the same time.

Figure 12.1

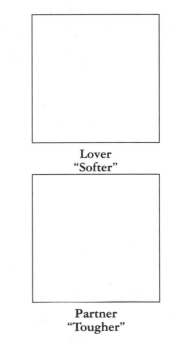

Lover
"Softer"

Partner
"Tougher"

Me
"Softer"

People often have an affair with someone who they believe will make up for their spouse's shortcomings. But they will never find what they're looking for until they make up for their *own* shortcomings. She needs to acquire *some* of what she complains about in her partner, and become a little "tougher," not find a "softer" partner. In many cases, this lets the marriage become truly *great*.

You describe yourself as on the "softer" side, whereas you describe your partner as more on the "tough" side. You were inexplicably drawn to this new flame because, "He was so emotionally available, and I was starving for connection and love. I didn't realize how lonely I'd become until I met him," you hear yourself say. Then you add, "If only my husband could be more like my lover without giving up his other good qualities!"

There it is, in Figure 12.1. But what is it a picture of? It doesn't describe all affairs, but it describes many. The flaw in the logic is my saying: "If I could just combine the traits of the two, I'd have the perfect partner." By saying this, I miss the fact that I'll never find that really great relationship until I acquire *some* of what I admire in my spouse! How's *that* for a brain-twister?! What's lacking in yourself is something that you originally tried to fill in by marrying your spouse in the first place. You weren't "tough," and so you admired your spouse's "toughness," "real-worldliness," "ability to make things happen and get things done," "assertiveness," "competence and effectiveness," "confidence in public," and so on.

If you are "too soft" and therefore don't relate well to your husband, one solution is to have an affair with someone who is "softer." But in most cases, that's a recipe for disaster. Another solution would be to *develop your "tough" or "realistic" side* just a bit more, because if you did, your husband would eventually be free to let his "soft" side out. Systems always strive for balance. The softer you become, the tougher he must become to achieve systemic balance. The tougher he becomes, the softer you become. But, if you become a little tougher, he will become a little softer.

Even if it ultimately turns out that you are married to the wrong person, you'll never have a relationship with a man who has a better balance of toughness and softness unless you create a better balance in yourself, first. No man with a healthier balance on that dimension would be interested in you until you did, because once you became romantically involved, the system the two of you created would be out of balance, like a seesaw with a much lighter person on one end. Systems strive for balance. And of course, it would all be unconscious— neither of you would be particularly aware that you were choosing or not choosing each other based on this balance.

So, suppose for a moment that you and your husband are *not a good fit,* and that your "ideal partner" is out there in the future. If you stay in a love triangle as a way to avoid the growing up that *you* need to do, then you'll never find him. That healthy grown-up woman or man "out there in your future" will not be attracted to the kind of conflicted, ambivalent people who inhabit prime-time soap operas. It is an act of fear and indecisiveness to be stringing two people along at the same time, not an act of integrity. *When people finally choose to stop using affairs as solutions to marital conflicts, they find out who they really are, who they really want, and then they start growing again.*

She (He) Knocked My Socks Off!

We recently heard a college professor on television say that "I was first attracted to her mind—the way she formulated her questions. I don't think physical attraction was *ever* a factor in our relationship. Our relationship is based on shared ideas."

Now, try the following "experiment." Think of all the couples you know, either personally or because they are public figures, and either look at them or at pictures of them, and then reflect for a moment on what score you would give each of them on a one-to-ten scale of attractiveness. We predict that with very few exceptions you will discover that people pair up with others who are just about equal to themselves on such a scale.

More controlled studies just like this have been done, with the very same results. In a typical experiment, photographs of couples who have been together long enough to be called "couples" are separated, and then a group of "man and woman on the street" raters are each asked to give a score to each photo on a scale from one to ten. The scores of each rater are combined to yield an average rating, which is then recorded for each photo. When each person's photo is then "reunited" with his partner's photo, it is discovered that in the vast majority of the pairings, the rating for one partner is within a point or two of the rating of the other partner in the couple. We pair up with people who are approximately as attractive as we are—the "eights" pair up with the "eights" and the "threes" pair up with the "threes." So, despite what the more intellectual and politically correct among us prefer to believe, the facts support the power of physical attraction in determining partner choice.

Physical attractiveness plays a very big role in countless aspects of life, from how we choose our partners to how long we stay in therapy, whether we get the job we interviewed for and the degree to which people believe us.[33] And of course, we can all think of examples where people who are quite far apart on attractiveness have been happily married for years. But if you also look at what factors determine how attractive a person appears, it still fits pretty well. Power makes someone appear more attractive than he or she may actually be. So do cultural norms, such as attractiveness of thin versus heavy people. In some South Pacific cultures, the heavier you are, the more influential you are, and therefore the more powerful and attractive you are. A powerful person who is just the "right" body mass for that particular culture will seem more attractive than he would seem if he wasn't as powerful or if he was of a different weight. We must also take into account the fact that as a group, women place less overall value on physical attractiveness than do men. But all in all, if you take these factors into account, then how people pair up with regard to attractiveness is pretty predictable.

There are less obvious factors that modulate perception of attractiveness, as well. The nonverbal messages that we give off—how we carry ourselves, whether we are loud or soft, funny or serious, and a whole host of other traits—all affect how attractive we are to others. These more subtle features can be potent determinants of our success in dating and mating rites. Imagine that you are at a large wedding reception, and across the room amid a sea of faces you spy an extremely attractive woman. She is stunning, breathtaking. You instantly notice that she is wound up like a spring about to snap, fidgeting, hyperactive, making extreme, unsophisticated, exaggerated gestures. Your heart stops doing its little pitter-patter and you resume your passage to the hors d'oeuvre table where you had spotted an old friend from college. The extremely attractive woman isn't potential dating material any longer.

If you are a fairly hyper person, then the chances are good that you will be "mysteriously" attracted to a person who is calm, understated and even-keeled. You might refer to her as having remarkable depth, poise and self-possession. If you are more of an introvert you could easily find yourself hopelessly in love with an energetic, outgoing, up-front woman whom you perceive as strong, confident and resilient. By the way, it is important to be mindful of the distinction between introversion and social fear. Introversion is a normal personality trait that describes a person who is more internally oriented, reflective and who probably prefers careers that allow quiet time and some solitude. If people terrify you, if you are frightened of social settings so much that you can barely negotiate them at all, then we may be talking about social anxiety disorder, which is something entirely different.

Can two extraverts be happy together? Certainly. Each pairing of people will create different challenges for the couple. Two introverts may struggle to stay connected enough and to create enough energy in the relationship, while two extraverts may have the problem of not enough depth or downtime for reflection and contemplation. After all, it is the extreme position on a given trait that typically causes trouble—extreme introverts can be withdrawn and reclusive, while extreme extraverts can be shallow, superficial and boorish.

No matter what it was that drew the two of you together, looking at what constituted that "initial magnetism" can be a revealing, and at times, entertaining exercise.

Patterns

People meet, fall in love and speak of each other as "soul mates" in the early months of their relationship. This feeling of "having known your lover forever" or "in another life" happens because the people we fall in love with *do* have characteristics of people from another life—that is, *the people from our childhoods.* While you will always be able to think of exceptions, we encourage you to look around and notice who is paired up with whom. Your partner may have the physical features of your mother or father—a narrow face, a round face, blonde hair, short stature, or more round and a bit on the heavy side. Even more so, your partner is likely to have personality characteristics that are similar to your mother or father—a perfectionist, possessing a temper, being forgetful about details, being intellectual and analytic, or being warm, nurturing and emotional. Or, they will have exactly the opposite characteristics—if we unconsciously choose a partner *as a reaction* to someone, our choice is still being determined by that someone.

A man whose father was passive, "too nice," and let himself get pushed around a lot may find himself marrying someone (1) whom he can push around a lot, or (2) who pushes him around a lot. A woman whose mother was warm and kind but overinvolved in her daughter's life may marry a man (1) who is either detached and aloof or (2) who smothers her with too much closeness.

A woman we know was raised by a kindhearted father who tended to push her a little too much to take physical risks that she didn't want to take, like skiing down a steeper-than-usual slope, or riding bicycles faster than she was comfortable doing. Eventually, she was quite able to say "no" to her father whenever he would suggest yet another "harebrained" scheme, but who did she marry? She married a man who tends to push her a little bit past her comfort level, which, interestingly, she acknowledges as both a positive as well as a negative factor in her life.

Some people are pleased to acknowledge that they married someone just like Dad. Some people aren't. Many men with whom we have worked had mothers who were emotionally unstable and highly volatile. Despite the fact that they tended to marry women who were like their mothers in certain ways, they struggled hard to avoid seeing that their partner choice had anything to do with their mothers. And why wouldn't they? Denial is a valuable, healthy defense mechanism. If I spent most of my childhood being burdened and overwhelmed by my mother, I will consciously need to tell myself that my choice of a partner has nothing to do with my mother. If I choose someone who is the exact opposite, then for sure I have avoided this mistake, right?

Other men had mothers who were adult women who were able to love their children in an uncomplicated way, with integrity and maturity. In that case, the choice of partners tends to be uncomplicated and clear—and healthy. We reenact whatever it was we grew up with. *Regardless of what we tell ourselves consciously, how we pick partners, and how we treat them and let them treat us, is determined long before we're adults.*

Bonding Patterns

Some people chuckle when they hear this lecture that we give, especially if we had just been talking about sexuality. We have to quickly clarify that we're talking about *"bonding"* not "bondage"!

Looking at the kinds of connections between family members can reveal a lot of clues about where your strengths and limitations are, especially if you are denying them for some reason. If blinders are originally installed for a good reason, then removing them will not always be easy. This is especially true for people when they look at these bonding patterns.

What we mean by a bond is some sort of *connection*. A connection is measured by *how much energy* is there, not by what kind of energy. If you feel close to Dad and want to be like him, that is one type of bond. If you are angry at Dad, and if the bitterness that you feel affects decisions that you make in your own life, then you are clearly bonded with him—it's just more of a negative bond. Until you are able to admit that in some ways you *are* like that parent, you will have trouble removing the blinders that you have about your own behavior. If you vowed *never* to be angry like your dad, and as a result, you are severely passive-aggressive in attempts to suppress your anger, then you may have a hard time seeing where the problem is.

We tell people that it usually takes one to two years to digest, integrate and apply this bonding information in their own lives, because while it is fairly easy to understand intellectually, it is quite a bit harder to apply to one's own situation. It is normal and healthy for every child in a family to want to be unique. But sometimes that uniqueness carries a price. Suppose you see your mother as sort of weak and helpless. You love her and appreciate her, but at one level you are also secretly annoyed that she doesn't stand up for herself more, especially to Dad. That's a fairly common scenario. Now, suppose that *you* are the one in the family who "takes on Dad." In his eyes, you're his Little Firecracker, and he is delighted with your spunk and verve. You won't put up with any of his domineering behaviors, and you won't back down when you believe you're right.

Some interesting things begin to develop. The more your position in the family solidifies, the more you find yourself pleased with your power, and the more you catch yourself alternating between feeling sorry for your mother and being angry at her for "not being the grown-up." The interesting question to ask yourself at this point is: Am I really more bonded to Dad? Or is a good chunk of my energy actually coming from my bond with Mom? Let's add one more fact—you're the second-born child in the family. You have an older brother and a younger brother and sister.

While it is not a hard and fast rule, the second child tends to have a little more of a bond with the mother, which could show up in several ways. You could have more conflict with Mom than anyone else in the family, especially during adolescence. You might carry her values or make life decisions in a similar fashion. You may be more accurately tuned to Mom and her feelings. After adolescence, even if you feel closer to Dad, you may still have one or two of Mom's primary, core traits, beliefs, strengths or limitations. Bonding connections result in our taking on one or more of the following: *behaviors, beliefs, feelings, attitudes, prejudices, strengths, limitations, worries, habits, interests, "life stance" or blinders.* Here is how the birth orders play out in *many* families:

First Child/Only Child: The first child has a little more of a connection with the father, and/or plays out the themes of the father a little more than the other children. As the Adlerians say, she tends to be more conforming and often more achievement-oriented. If the family carries a distinct split between the overt and covert rules ("all Smiths are honest, God-fearing folk" vs. "but we are pretty dishonest in our business dealings," or "we are not very emotionally honest"), this will be very apparent in the first child, who, in the above example, will be an honest, God-fearing person who isn't very honorable in his business dealings but somehow separates that from the rest of his life, or who is honest in business but lacks an equal amount of honesty in his emotional life. The latter might show up as fear of vulnerability resulting in strong defensiveness around and denial of his "softer" emotions. First children also tend to be more rational and less affected by emotions.

Second Child: The second child plays out the themes of the mother, and like a lot of mothers, tends to pay more attention to others' emotional needs. They often feel like they don't have much influence on the family, and so one of their issues will be to learn how to acquire and use healthy power. As described above, some second children do not want to acknowledge that they have a connection to Mom because they perceive Mom to be overly vulnerable or ineffective in the family. Second children who are particularly angry fit this scenario. Many more second children are very pleased to acknowledge that they have many of Mom's traits or core approaches to life. As with all birth orders, it is important for second children to acknowledge both the strengths as well as the limitations of that parent or part of the system, and see where his or her blinders might be, as a result.

Third Child: The third child is a mirror for the parents' marital relationship. Because this is a more abstract connection than a bond with a single person, third children tend to look at the more abstract aspects of life and to miss the details and particulars. They are often more interested in theories than facts, in other words. Because they are bonded with the marital relationship, they tend to focus on relationships outside the family, too. They are often the ones running around the college dorms, trying to help put others' relationships back together again, but having trouble themselves with their own separate identities. They get caught in triangles more than others and, while they seem to be detached from others, are actually very emotionally involved.

Fourth Child: The fourth child's connection is even more abstract than the third. As in a regression equation or an analysis of variance, the "Dad stuff" is taken by the first child, the "Mom-stuff" is taken by the second, the "Marital-stuff" is taken by the third and so the "variance" remaining for the fourth child to claim is the "Family System-stuff." Fourth children are often unaware that they are like "tuning forks" for the system. We have had fourth children tell us that when they go home to big holiday family get-togethers, as soon as they walk through the door they start to feel anxious and agitated, responding to all of the covert messages and tensions that are constantly flashing between family members. They can feel the ancient, simmering hurt and anger between Grandpa and Aunt Kathleen, and the jealousy felt by Tim as he feels a triangle developing between him, his sister Susan and his sister Arlene. Fourth children are often the keepers of the family rules, too. When someone suggests that for a change we all spend Hanukkah at Aunt Sarah's rather than at Grandma Ruth's, the fourth child will often protest loudly, saying, "We *always* spend the holiday at Grandma Ruth's. We *can't* change that tradition!"

Fifth/Sixth/Etc.: Because all of the "variance" in the family system has been accounted for, when a fifth child comes along, he or she starts back at the beginning, with more of a connection to, or playing out the themes of, Dad. The sixth would be bonded with Mom, and on it goes.[34]

While these patterns do not fit all families, and while they are certainly hard to unearth in blended families or in the case of adoption, they do have an uncanny degree of consistency—but only if you are able to look beneath the surface of your preconceived notions about the person with whom you believe you are like or unlike. And remember, the value of understanding your bonding patterns is in *understanding yourself and in removing one or two of your blinders.*

We once had a client who was very annoyed by our suggestion, several months into therapy, that because he was the first child he might be playing out some of his father's themes or behaviors. He protested vigorously. We said that was okay, we didn't have any big investment in him fitting some theoretical pattern, and that this stuff wasn't absolute law. But we wondered if he saw how he was like his father, and we were concerned because he had some of the traits that he had described his father as having, but his were masked by some subtle, covert defenses. He had a tendency to make sarcastic little jabs that were delivered with a smile and followed by a choppy "heh heh heh." These features were combined in just the right way that the result often felt like an attack.

Rather than fighting with him about it, we said it wasn't that important. As we began to move on in the session, we tossed in as an almost absentminded aside that if he had a relative who lived in another part of the country and who knew the family but had some distance from the family as well, he might want to call that person and just ask. We saw a flicker of interest in his eyes as we proceeded to the next issue in the session. Two weeks later he walked into the office with an indescribably whimsical expression on his face. After our initial check-in, he said that he had something to share.

"I have an aunt in New Orleans who is eighty-four years old," he said excitedly. "I kept thinking about what you had suggested about me and my father, and I got madder and madder and more and more intrigued at the same time. It was like there was a battle going on inside of me between two separate armies. So I called her up last week. She knows the family well, but she only gets together with the family maybe once every five years. So I said that my 'crazy' therapists had suggested that I might somehow be like my father—but that I'm not like him at all. I have been closer to my mother for as long as I can remember. And if I'm bonded with anyone, it's with Uncle Frank," I told her.

"And?"

"There was a pause at the other end of the line, and then she asked me if I wanted to know if I was at all like my dad."

"And then?"

"I said 'Yes,' and then she burst into waves of uproarious laughter!"

"That's amazing."

"It *is* amazing! She went right down a list of characteristics, from mannerisms and figures of speech, to political beliefs, to pet peeves. And *then* she got more serious and talked to me very calmly and supportively about what you have called my sarcastic barbs. She said they were often cruel, and that while she knew I didn't mean any harm by them, she had seen them cut, over the years, at various family get-togethers. And then she said that my father's defensiveness was from a lot of hurt that happened to him, and that she hoped I could release some of that defensiveness in myself, because I was pushing people away with it, just like Dad. It was astonishing."

Knowing who you are and with whom you were bonded as a child is one of the best ways to understand why you chose to be in love with the person you chose. You may have been protective of Mom when you were little, and you may have vowed not to be like Dad when you grew up. But that doesn't mean you created a marriage that is much different than your parents' marriage. When you remove those blinders, you can see how you chose your wife in the first place, how she chose you, and how you *are* hurting her, rather than how you *are not* hurting her. And then you can change. After all, how you are not hurting her doesn't matter, does it? What matters is how you *are* hurting her.

Painting a Picture and Coming Out of the Fog

In the final section of this chapter, we want to take you through a small part of the clinical process that many people find helpful as they begin to look at how they create the marriages that they do. In Figure 12.2, we have reproduced in abbreviated form a genogram—a family map—that we sometimes use in therapy. It can get complicated trying to explain the details of how these patterns play out, and sometimes the best way to help people understand what the playing field really looks like is to draw it on paper. The family displayed here is an actual family, and the descriptions are the actual words used by the person whom we helped construct this genogram. What might be a little misleading is that the insights and awarenesses that are summarized in this genogram were gradually added to it over a period of many months, rather than in one or two sessions. Our genograms are always a work in progress as long as we continue to mature and deepen over the years.

Tom, we'll call him, a high-powered, successful executive, had been referred by his employer, although he joked comfortably during the first session that if his employer hadn't sent him, his wife would have—indeed, she was ready to initiate a trial separation if things didn't start changing at home. He said that his employer had sent him because of his anger, and that his wife's complaint was the same. We asked if he'd ever hit his wife or children or people at work, and he said he hadn't. He said his anger came out mostly in being "prickly." He was unduly critical, perfectionistic, condescending, snapped at people and was uncomfortably gruff, so that the people closest to him felt like they were walking on eggshells when around him. He was willing to admit that he had a problem and that he could no longer deny it because he was getting feedback about it from all corners of his universe.

Over the ensuing months, Tom gradually filled in his family map. He didn't know much about his grandparents on his mother's side, and he'd never given that fact much thought. As we grow up, we tend to accept as "normal" whatever it was we grew up with. For example, men who were beaten by their fathers when they were children will

Figure 12.2

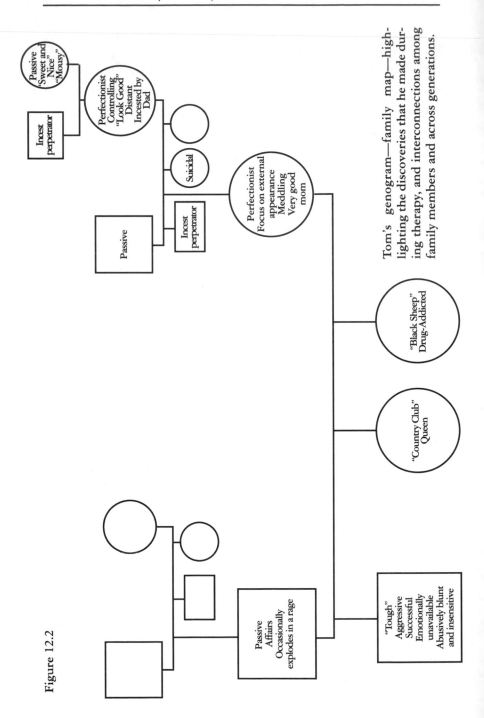

Tom's genogram—family map—highlighting the discoveries that he made during therapy, and interconnections among family members and across generations.

often say, "That's the way kids were raised back then. All my friends' dads gave them a beating now and then, too. It was the norm." Tom didn't know much about his maternal grandparents because his mother and father didn't tell any stories about them. For the same reason, he didn't know much about his mother's childhood, either. He *did* know that when he was growing up, his mother had been "a very good mom—she was always baking, sewing, making sure we ate well and were dressed well and did well in school— you know, just a regular old, good mother."

Of course, each of us goes into adulthood with an interpreted image of our childhood and our parents that is much more like an impressionistic painting than a photograph. Tom had initially described his sister as a "country club queen," which he said with a faint hint of contempt rather than gentle good humor. We asked how he meant that, just to be sure we weren't misinterpreting his words. He said that she seemed more concerned with status and image than he would prefer. He belonged to the country club set, he added, but it was different—he wasn't imprisoned by the need to appear a certain way or to fit in, the way he perceived his sister to be.

We then asked him if his mother had been focused on how the family looked and his eyes lit up for a moment. "Oh, yes." He let out a long breath of emphasis on the first word. "Yes. Sometimes it felt like we were little puppets in her private play. Every Sunday morning was the mad dash to get the four of us dressed, my two sisters' hair perfect, our shirts starched and spotless, shoes shined. She would bark out commands like a marine corps drill sergeant, and my father and we kids would scurry around like church mice until we passed muster, and then off we'd go. The car was spotless. Mom looked perfect. It felt like all heads turned and all eyes were riveted to the six of us as we paraded into church just at the right time, filled the left half of the long pew, and then held our breaths for sixty minutes as the service progressed. Then we all marched out, watched as Mom and Dad greeted their friends, and then it was home, where we could finally exhale and claim the rest of the day as our own."

"It sounds like your mother was very organized and detail-oriented," we offered, being careful not to overinterpret his description, which could force him into feeling like he had to defend his family rather than form a clearer picture of it for himself.

Instead of tossing out another throwaway joke, he looked thoughtfully at the emerging picture on the flipchart and said, "I think I resented her for that more than I've been willing to admit. She was such a good mom in so many ways, but something was missing." He looked sad for a fleeting moment, and then continued. "I just wish I'd had some *time* with her—you know, time just to hang out and be. My good friend in grammar school had a mom like that, and I was secretly envious of him."

"What was your friend's mother like?" we asked.

"Oh, she did all those good things moms do—the cooking and cleaning and so on—but she'd slow down now and then, and she wasn't constantly correcting and improving and adjusting everything about her kids the way my mother did. This kid's dad was the tougher one, I guess."

"Have you ever asked your mother what her childhood was like? What she liked to do, who her friends were? What her family did on weekends, on vacations? Have you ever tried to fill in some of the details?"

"I need to do that." He was quiet.

"It's good to have a clear picture of things."

Several months later, after some pretty focused "here-and-now" work on his anger at home and at work, he came in with a countenance we had never seen on his face. He said that he had talked with his mother at length during his recent business trip to Cleveland, where she lives. He said it was a life-altering experience, and that he had some things to add to his genogram. He began, "I wasn't angry. I was curious. I was interested in her story for its own sake, the way you have been interested in mine. She must have sensed that, and she must have been ready to unburden herself. Because it was stunning."

"What did you discover?" we asked.

"First off, I wasn't sure of her birth order when we first started doing this genogram. It turns out that she has an older brother and two younger sisters."

"She's a second child," we noted.

"Yes. She started to describe her older brother, my uncle, who I rarely ever saw when I was growing up, and her lip started to quiver. She said that he had sexually abused one of his daughters and that the entire family kept it a secret. Then she wept openly."

"It sounds like a very powerful moment for both you and your mother."

"Yes," he continued. "But what *really* got me was what

came next. Through her sobs, she shared that her father had incested *her* from the time she was seven until she was thirteen, and that he'd done it to her two sisters, too." Tom's voice cracked and tears welled up in his eyes. "She was *so* vulnerable, so old, so ashamed. My strong, powerful, controlling, perfectionistic mother. It was . . . it was . . . *so* . . . painful."

"It was such a gift for both of you. Sometimes life is so beautiful and so unbearably painful at the same moment that it escapes our comprehension."

"Yes. It is such a relief to know this. I always knew somewhere deep in my heart that there was a big piece of the picture that was missing. This explains so much."

"Everyone in a family has a unique vantage point. No matter how many people are looking at a family from how many angles, no one can ever see the whole picture. Families are simply too complex. What did you see at that moment in time?"

"I saw a little girl, terrified, ashamed, betrayed by her father and mother, going to school each day, carrying a horrible secret, trying to maintain the semblance of normalcy in her deranged world, and becoming more and more numb with every passing day."

"Exactly," we agreed.

"No wonder she became so controlling!"

"It was one of the few sane options open to her as she was enduring that," we added, knowing that it was both true, as well as important to emphasize when there is so much shame and anxiety bubbling up at one time.

"You're right," Tom said, calmer now. "What else could a

little child do in a situation like that? She was too little to run away from home."

"Some children do, but their lives are so fragile at seven or eight."

"Yes. Their lives are so fragile at seven or eight. God!" He began to cry some more. "It's a wonder she didn't commit suicide."

"Children do."

"I am so glad I had that conversation with her."

"How did it end? Where did the two of you leave it?"

"It ended surprisingly well. She felt better; I felt better. She didn't have to avoid eye contact." He chuckled warmly. "No. That's certainly not *my* mother's weak suit—she's not one to let things keep her down for long."

"So even though she was a vulnerable child, she developed a strong, clear spirit?" we asked.

"Yes. She has pissed me off more times than I could count because of her dominating ways, but after all is said and done, her strengths far outweigh her limitations."

"Indeed," we continued. "By the way, what did you find out about *her* mother?"

"She described her mother as sort of 'mousy' and ineffectual. She wondered if she was so controlling to make up in part for her mother's seeming lack of control over her own life. She also said that her sister closest to her in age had been suicidal on and off during her teens and twenties, and she thought her other sister had been treated for depression at various times throughout her life."

"Did she think her mother knew about the incest?"

"A word about it was never spoken between them, but

she sensed that her mother knew and was too ashamed and afraid to do or say anything."

"That's a pretty common reaction," we replied.

"She must have hated her father at some level. And her mother, too, for letting it happen."

"It's so complex, isn't it? Parents are parents, so we need them and love them no matter what they do. Her feelings for her father and mother must be very conflicted," we said, creating a clear opening for him to see more details of the picture. "Her ambivalence must be exquisite."

"As is mine," he smiled, thoughtfully.

"Of course it is. How could it not be? Do you think you are an angry person? Do you believe there's some truth to all of the complaints people at home and at work have been making?"

"Oh, sure. I mean, I can see a big difference already in how people behave around me since you and I have been working on my anger these past few months. I can see that I've been a jerk in many ways."

"Why do you think you have that subtle contempt for your sister? The one you call the country club queen?"

"Because she's such a damned phony."

"Is she focused a lot on appearances?"

"It's sad, really. It's as if she spends every waking moment plagued by this terrible dread that someone might actually find out that she's a human being. The end result is that she's shallow and superficial and obsessed with external perfection, but hollow and empty inside."

"She's the second-born child."

"And?"

"The second-born child plays out the themes and/or patterns of the mother. All four of you children were affected by both of your parents in various ways, but the second child has a unique connection with the mother."

"My wife is a second-born, but she was much closer to her father."

"Feeling closer to her father is different than playing out the patterns and/or themes of her mother. In any event, in your sister's case, this birth order effect is pretty clear."

"Yes. You're right." Tom stared silently at the now quite complex genogram on the flipchart in our office. Several seconds passed. "As I reflect on Mom, I am able to make her more than one-dimensional now, even though I'm sure her good old defenses kicked in right after I left Cleveland."

"Probably did."

"But she showed me something of her true self. She was so vulnerable, without being helpless. All of those emotions that I once thought were negative—fear, hurt, shame, loneliness, anger—came pouring out, and I left Cleveland with a three-dimensional relationship with her."

"*Is* your sister like your mother?"

"Yes. And my contempt comes from . . . from . . . ," he was groping for the word.

"Your loneliness?" we offered.

"Yes. I was *unknowingly* angry at my mother, and *openly* angry with my sister, because that emphasis on appearances left me feeling so alone. Yet, when I look at this entire picture all at once, rather than feeling *angry* because I was alone, I feel *compassion* and *understanding* for my mother and why she chose to put so much emphasis on how her family looked—she was so shame-filled and burdened with that horrible secret. She was doing what a strong little girl would do in order to survive. It's not just that she did the best she could, and then moved on. It's that she did the best she could, it makes sense why she did it, and she also had tremendous strength, character, love and care that she expressed in her way as opposed to mine. I can be angry at her for being emotionally remote and controlling and per-fectionistic, *and* I can be grateful that she is my mother, and love her, all in the same moment."

Life is so much simpler when we let all of it in. Tom had assembled enough of the puzzle pieces to give him a glimpse of the whole picture, which is infinitely rewarding in its own right. We all sat there in silence for a few seconds to let it sink in, and then we asked, "And what about your sister?"

"You know, I may never be able to have the kind of break-through with her that I just had with Mom. If I do, it would be a gift. But if I don't, this work removes so much of the negative energy from my relationship with her. I think I can interact with her without being as much of a jerk as I have been in the past."

"So this is really back to being about you and not about what's wrong with everyone else?"

"Yes."

"And what do you see in your marriage?"

"That's the best of all. I see why I picked Joan in the first place. She was softer and kinder than me. I was able to run roughshod over her in the beginning, but she was also able to give me a lot of the warmth and affection that my mother wasn't able to. But beneath it all, she has the strength of my mother, because she finally put her foot down with me and said, 'You start dealing with your anger, or else.' That she was warm and loving and caring allowed me to believe that even though she meant it, I had a chance to save our marriage—that she'd be there for me 100 percent if I changed."

"You picked someone softer, like your father, but also determined and clear, like your mother."

"Yes."

13

Let Yourself Be Astonished

Ishmael gave himself to the writing of it, and as
he did so he understood this, too: that accident
ruled every corner of the universe except the
chambers of the human heart.

—David Guterson
Snow Falling on Cedars

How astonishing it is to be a small but integral part of
a universe, in which, by your simple connection to humanity, you find your spirit rising and your tears flowing
through the voice of a Luciano Pavarotti, a Paul McCartney
or an Ella Fitzgerald. What an honor to be a member of the
human race, and to thus be able to identify with the
Gandhis and the Dorothy Days of the world. It is astonish-
ingly simple, like breathing.

How does anyone convey the profound value of the

185

ordinary in everyday life? With poetry? In a song? A painting? By example? A talented literary writer can do it. We've seen it in those rare, unforgettable moments in remarkable films. There are certain lives that, like the best prayers, embody it effortlessly.

The more deeply connected we become with the innermost edges and corners of our souls, the more we are able to appreciate the ordinary aspects of life. One of the true joys of being an adult is the ability to appreciate the simple fact of being alive. It is not trite. People who have this ability have earned it, for it does not come easily. A woman who experienced tremendous tragedy in her life came to make sense of its nuances and meanings and messages, and ultimately said, "I have seen so much sorrow in my life, but I have endured; and now it is a smile, a tear, a bird singing and the very light of day that warms my heart. My life is blessed beyond measure."

It is easy to talk about the importance of simple astonishment, but it is another thing to embrace it and work it into one's being. Many of us still seem to cling to the notion that we can have it all, and if we don't, we complain about our unhappiness. Many of us take each other for granted as we strive to acquire more and more of something, anything, that we believe will make us just a little bit happier than the next person. A bigger house, perhaps? A new spouse? Different friends? An exciting new vacation spot that nobody else has heard of yet? We are on never-ending spiritual quests as if our established institutions had suddenly been drained of their wisdom by some mysterious force.

The true road to spiritual excellence, to which so many

contemporary adults aspire, is a simple one. How many times have we heard that? There are so many self-help regimens out there. So much wisdom, repeated so often, that it loses its "Oompf!" Simplify, simplify, simplify, we hear, but the sheer volume of messages coming into our homes and offices is so large that the thought of simplifying our lives is overwhelming because we don't know which parts to simplify! As we hurtle recklessly down the freeway talking on our cell phones and narrowing our coronary arteries with excessive stress, we are encouraged to *"chop wood, carry water."* What a conundrum.

On a Flight to Tokyo

What might happen if you turned off all the noise for a few moments and just listened to the hum of the universe pulsing all around you? We *are* tuning forks after all, and each of us has a range of resonances to which we are tuned. What is it that I might pick up if I were just the slightest bit more mindful, intentional, present and sensory?

I might think of you and remember that when you smile, your eyes crinkle up at the outside corners in a way that makes my heart skip a beat. I might notice that the Japanese man across the aisle from me is weeping at the poignant moment in the film[35] when David Duchovny pulls up on the bicycle with the nun riding on the handlebars and tells Minnie Driver that he loves her, right in the middle of a crowded Italian piazza. I might notice that it feels good to shed tears at moments like these, and to know that even two thousand miles out over the Pacific Ocean, in a cramped coach seat on a 747 headed for Tokyo, little moments can happen. They aren't confined to a certain time, place or circumstance.

If I keep the noise tuned out for a few more moments I might imagine the Pacific Ocean thirty-five thousand feet below and how entranced I have always been by it—by its dark blue depths, the way the sun plays off it so differently from moment to moment to moment from first light till last. I might recall the time my sister and I almost drowned in fifteen-foot waves while bodysurfing off the northwest corner of Oahu, and how she meant well when she was so excited the first time I got married at the age of twenty, but how grateful I am for the marriage that I have today. I might remember the old Victorian mansions that my wealthy friends lived in, or that their grandparents lived in, just north of San Francisco, where the fog excuses itself from duty more often than not. I might remember the unbeliev-able, heart-stopping magic of a friend and I discovering a Model-T Ford or an old Packard hidden away in one of those dilapidated wooden garages with the dirt or timber-planked floors, the exterior shrouded in vines and tree branches that should have been pruned ages ago.

I might remember the sweet, pungent, musty smell of old engine oil and dirt and sun-bleached wood and the dampness captured by the roots and the terrified awe when we'd flip over one of those planks quickly enough to see a centipede racing away, its bright yellow-orange exterior and its nasty-looking red legs creating an indelible image on the backs of our retinas.

For a moment I might think about the pain and fear and

pounding of my heart that came when my parents fought late at night, and in the next moment I would be in the two-tone 1953 Plymouth sedan riding through the New Mexico desert at sunrise, four years old, on a magical family journey. Then I might smell fresh spring rain, hear rushing water through redwood and bay laurel, feel mud, and whiff the beckoning call of my mother's freshly baked apple pie made with golden delicious apples from the tree in our backyard. They would be the same apples that our cocker spaniel/toy-shepherd mix would munch on reflectively while lying under that tree on a hot, dry, lazy summer afternoon. From there, I might see a family of California quail scurrying across the lawn and into the hydrangeas or I might hear the yelping of five-day-old puppies in their "nest" with their mother, next to the warmth emanating from the motor of the old refrigerator in a quiet corner of the little kitchen.

Then I would remember how hard my father worked to build his career and to provide for us, and how dedicated he was to being on the school board and to coaching Little League baseball and to taking his sons duck hunting and trout fishing and hiking. But if I go there, then I am confronted by my longstanding resistance to giving my mother anywhere near the credit she deserves for the Herculean expenditure of effort that she put into caring for and raising us, from the lovingly prepared and most competent of meals to the endless driving over Mt. Tamalpais to the beach and what must have been the nerve-fraying stress of mediating the conflict and sibling rivalry of three overactive children, all the while being the daughter and wife of an alcoholic and going through menopause, a hysterectomy, and her own marital heartaches and personal demons while trying to be the best wife and mother she could be, and being treated like all "neurotic" housewives of the 1950s by being given and becoming addicted to dangerous prescription drugs like barbiturates, amphetamines and tranquilizers.

I would then catch myself being ever so grateful for all of those incredible meals, all of those magical trips to the beach, all of those vacations to Lake Tahoe and Utah and New Mexico that went without a hitch, during which time we just took for granted that there would be a "mom" there managing everything flawlessly. That she burned herself out by trying too hard detracts not one iota from the gratitude that I feel. The fact that she tended to be overly emotional does not diminish how hard it must have been, as my wife so compassionately points out, to not be taken seriously enough by her husband and children when it came to "unimportant things" like the upkeep of the house itself, the occasional upgrading of the furnishings within, or the crack in the foundation that after all was said and done did indeed threaten the safety of everyone it supported. But then, that was ignored until after they both died and the house was put up for sale.

Now, if I choose to be still and listen just a few moments longer, and because our realities and our existence are in many ways timeless, I might then leap back into the present as if jumping into a wormhole in deep space, and realize how grateful I am for the impeccable taste that my wife has, for how she has done battle with me without giving up or giving in when her own inner voice so directed her; for how feminine she is and how powerful she is, and for how our lives have blended together around certain themes and activities and habits in such a way that, if she were to die, the hole that would be left would be like the meteor crater in the Arizona desert that my brother and sister and I marveled at when we were little, and how it would ache as much as that crater is deep and wide.

The Yippy Little Dog

On a cold, cloudy Saturday morning I could wake up and look over at your tousled hair, partially covered by the sheet that you pulled across it in the middle of the night, then I could turn and see that little dog of ours, on his side, his head laying on the end of my pillow, his body stretched straight behind his head, his legs gently tucked in, so he looks like the little person he is. Then, right there on that dreary, unremarkable winter morning, my mind might flash to a composite picture of a lonely little girl standing sadly at her bedroom window after school, looking down at the street, waiting with hope of all hopes for the mailman to bring her the puppy she wanted so badly, to ease her loneliness. She had filled an envelope with all of her pennies and nickels and dimes and mailed it to the pet store, and knew that certainly the puppy would come. But it never did.

When you wake up and we both laugh as our dog rolls over on his back and luxuriates in the sheer joy of being a Saturday morning bum, I remember back the eight short years to the day that I, like your mean father, said, "What do you want to get a puppy for? We're going on vacation in ten days. Who will take care of it?" You said we were going to look at puppies, and that was that, and for some reason I just settled down and went. You were too powerful at that moment. I might remember that when we brought him home, our big dog gave him a bad time at first, and then a few days later, she accidentally broke his leg while they were roughhousing. As you pulled into the driveway you saw me standing there, holding him in my hand, his left hind leg dangling like a piece of spaghetti. Your heart sunk for a moment. You thought I was going to say that we'd have to put him to sleep.

As I jumped in the car to rush him to the vet, you realized that I had fallen in love with the little guy as much as you, despite my earlier belief that "all little dogs are dumb and yippy." You held him in your arms until we got there. He was partially in shock, moaning quietly. He turned out to be the biggest trouper in the whole family, racing around with his leg bone surgically pinned and wrapped tightly in a long bandage that was the equivalent of a cast. He was and still is the cutest little guy in the world. I hate to think what we would have missed had you listened to me grumbling about "yippy little dogs" and "going on vacation soon." He has graced our life in ways that would have been impossible for me to imagine had I even tried, and I hadn't. I thank you for being strong enough to stand up to me, and for being so patient, determined and intuitive to know that, forty years later, nothing would do except to finally get that little dog, once and for all.

He has been everything and more of the companion that you have always wanted—laying on the bed with you day after day after day while you recuperated from that brutal surgery is only one of hundreds of examples. As I watched him grow up, I watched you walk him and bathe him and rock him in the rocking chair, holding him in your arms on his back so he would learn to trust—which he certainly has, and in a most remarkable way. And as I saw how much healing of your old wounds was quietly taking place because you finally *did* get that dog that you used to wait for every day after school, tears came to my eyes and my heart leaped with joy. And my soul deepened, too. What a gift he has been to both of us. There is awe and wonder and astonishment all around us, all of the time. We just have to be open to it.

Karl Rahner

There are countless people whose very lives are sources of wonder and astonishment, too. When our clients are having difficulty finding the goodness and value in humanity, we encourage them to think of their personal heroes, and if they have none, we prime the pump by recalling one or two of our own, and our reasons for the choices. Mother Teresa and Nelson Mandela come to mind, as do Abraham Lincoln, Eleanor Roosevelt, Marie Curie and Albert Einstein.

If someone says, "Yeah, well, *they* had special gifts and were unique," we note that when Mother Teresa was asked by a reporter what it was like to be called a living saint, she replied that:

> *You have to be holy in your position, as you are. And I have to be holy in the position that God has put me. So it is nothing*

extraordinary to be holy. Holiness is not the luxury of the few. Holiness is a simple duty for you and for me. We have been created for that.[36]

Awe and wonder and astonishment are not confined to the fortunate few who make their living looking at the stars through the telescopes on Mauna Kea or Mt. Palomar, or who become the leaders who save the world from itself. They are for everyone.

We are reminded of German priest Karl Rahner, who is typically described as the leading Catholic theologian of the twentieth century. Rahner spoke of spirit as the "unutterable mystery," but he also said that:

. . . the experience of spirit is given to us, even though we usually overlook it in the pursuit of our everyday lives, and perhaps repress it and do not take it seriously enough. . . .[37]

It is not a surprising statement coming from a man whose original doctoral thesis in philosophy was rejected as too radical. He went on to develop a style of reconciliation in his writings which would bring his message of openness to even the most conservative of his peers through exhaustive research and attention to detail in portraying the development of dogma. He was chosen by many of the cardinals at the Second Vatican Council as their chief theological advisor and was ultimately responsible for the Church's newfound openness to different religions, and to the belief that God's salvation is for everybody.[38]

Like many truly great people, he was not just a great thinker. During World War II, he served as a parish priest in Innsbruck, Austria, where he also spent the last thirteen years of his life ministering to the people in his parish. In fact, a man we know was going through a particularly difficult time back in the 1970s, and had grown to admire the writings and thinking of Rahner. Seeking comfort from this connection, the man, who lived here in the United States, sent a letter to Rahner, realizing that he would most likely never get a reply from such a famous man. Several months later, the man received a handwritten reply from Rahner—dated only one day after Rahner had received it—much to his awe and astonishment. It turns out that this brilliant theologian and distinguished lecturer lived what he taught. Despite his world renown and busy schedule, he apparently answered every letter that was sent to him, in addition to ministering to all of his parishioners in Innsbruck on a daily basis.

Rahner was the living, breathing embodiment of how spirituality is present in each of us, regardless of our professed beliefs. In summarizing Rahner's theology of Jesus Christ in Boston University's *Dictionary of Modern Western Theology,* JeeHo Kim wrote: "[According to Rahner] . . . Christians can learn from other religions or atheistic humanism because God's grace is . . . operative in them (Schineller 1991, p. 102). Christ is present and operative in and through his Spirit."

It is awe inspiring in itself to trace the complex theological reasoning that Rahner had to develop in order to convince modern theologians of the simple truth that Jesus Christ lived every day, which is that everyone is to be included—prostitutes, gamblers, intellectuals, holy men, beggars—everyone. Today, it is a contentious and convoluted question as to whether non-Christians can be "saved." Rahner presented three very clear, sound requirements for how anyone can be included in Christ's salvation. To do so, we must carry in our hearts the following three attitudes:

1. An absolute love toward neighbors
2. An attitude of readiness for death
3. An attitude of hope for the future

Rahner's explanation is intellectually brilliant, possesses emotional integrity, is intuitively sensible and is elegant. In other words, it is awe inspiring.

He chose the arena of theological politics, for lack of a better term, in which to carry out his life's work. He believed that Jesus Christ's message was simple, inclusive and left no room for intolerance, fear or hatred of others. But you can't just say that to a two-thousand-year-old church hierarchy and expect everyone to heartily agree. In two thousand years, anyone's original message is going to become blurred. Karl Rahner used his intelligence, his conviction, his sense of what was right and the goodness of his soul to help turn an ocean liner with a paddle. And in our opinion, when he was done, the ship was headed back in the direction it was originally headed, two thousand years ago.

There is something awe inspiring about a great man or woman who maintains his or her perspective in the world and therefore remains genuinely humble in the experience of greatness. To watch someone be profoundly creative and innovative amid the fears of those trying to protect the established order—in other words, to be *respectfully restive*—and to remain committed to helping those innovations become part of the establishment is awesome to behold.

As all of the great people mentioned above either said directly or implied by the way they lead their lives, astonishment, spirituality and greatness "are not the luxury of the few"—they belong to each of us. Between our birth and our death lies the space in which we each can exercise that greatness and experience that wonder in the universe around us, in our own unique ways.

Have We Lost the Capacity for Awe?

The two reflections at the very beginning of this chapter were triggered by a brief moment of stillness and intentional perception—what we have long called *Noticing and Listening*. It isn't expensive. It uses up hardly any precious time at all. And yet, if you were to do a little bit of this every day, especially if you were adept at the kind of "time travel" described above, imagine how it might deepen your love and appreciation for your life, the people in it and, especially, your partner.

For many years, we have connected the ability to have awe and wonder about the universe with our capacity for spirituality. The partial loss of the openness to be astonished is one of the saddest developments of late twentieth-century America. Many people are concerned that excessive materialism and the disconnection from one another that is exacerbated by computers and video games and destructively hectic schedules are killing our souls. At times, there does seem to be more jadedness, callousness and indifference, especially to the little tragedies and triumphs all around us. Maybe it's the media's emphasis on the sensational story—negative stories are usually more sensational than inspiring ones. Maybe it's the overstimulation—too much stimulation deadens the brain's reaction to things. Or maybe it's a combination of these.

And maybe because of all those stressors, we've simply lost the ability to make the finer discriminations that people used to make—the ability to discern the difference between a made-for-television movie and a Shakespearean play, between disappointment and sadness, between the Japanese culture and the Chinese culture, between clean water and polluted water. We speak of taking life for granted. Of passing by the sacred as we hurry across a crowded intersection on the way to work and not even knowing it, as Karl Rahner implied. Of the power of accepting the ordinariness of real spirituality. Of the paradox of depth through simplicity—of things becoming more complex and therefore simpler.

Spiritual Bankruptcy and Spiritual Grace

Spirituality is our ability to delight in the complexity and vastness of the night sky one moment, and then in the next, to marvel at the power and elegance of a virus that has morphed and evolved over millions of years. Spirituality is also the ability to surrender to the occasional unique brutalities that are an unavoidable part of life for each of us.

Having a curious mind, a sharp eye, a precisely tuned ear—
these are what permit us to connect with the world around
us in much more than just physical ways. When we pay
attention to the teeming life around us, the messages are
there.

In *The 7 Best Things (Smart) Teens Do,* we described two
women who, when compared to each other, create a stark
contrast between spiritual bankruptcy and the awe-
inspiring power of spirit and grace. We would like to share
these two stories with you in the hope that in their point
and counterpoint, they will allow you to glimpse yet
another facet of the magic in relationships.

The Media Rep[39]

"I kicked their asses!" gloated Sandra Hart in April 1995.
A renowned public-relations executive, she had been picked
up by the Minneapolis police who thought they had run
across a "slumper," that is, a drunk driver who had pulled
over in her car and fallen asleep or passed out. When her case
came up before Judge Myron Greenberg, he regretfully dis-
missed it because of technicalities. Hart had a long history of
alcohol-related driving arrests and convictions, but claimed
that they had all occurred in the 1970s. Of course, the record
showed otherwise. She had actually been arrested for drunk
driving in 1981, 1983, 1984, 1988, twice in 1990 and again
in 1993. When she commented on the judge's reluctant decision, she crowed, "I kicked their asses! I was never afraid or
fearful. I had two things on my side: God and the justice
system."

God? The *Nazis* thought they had God on their side. The *Ku Klux Klan* thinks they have God on their side. *We* thought we had God on our side when we tried to carpet bomb Vietnam into oblivion. And now this woman thinks that *she* has God on her side? When a parent slaps a child across the face and blackens his eye, the parent will often explain it by saying that he had to do it "for the child's own good," which may sound plausible to some people at first glance, but of course, it is pitifully implausible. There is no research, experience or wisdom to support the goodness of such an act. But we humans have a peculiar habit of believing that what we do must be right by the simple fact that we did it. We tend to be pretty narcissistic.

Another strange thing that we human beings do is that many of us have a strong tendency to actually pity—to feel sorry for and protect—people who do cruel, terrible things. At some level we detect how damaged a person must be to treat others that way, and so the compassionate part of us tries to take over from the wise part of us.

When we recount the details of the above incident involving Sandra Hart to audiences of professionals who are attending a training seminar on working with victim-perpetrator dynamics, their immediate reaction is shock and disgust. As we interact more with the audience, asking questions and probing a bit beneath the surface, what everyone discovers is that every person's inner reaction to things is not always the same as his or her surface reaction. For example, people who are angry at the law or at bureaucrats or at their parents or at the government may find themselves secretly applauding this woman's actions. People who are alcoholic or drug-addicted—yes, there are psychologists, psychiatrists, social workers and counselors who are—may feel unconsciously protective of this woman because they share an addiction in common. People who were intimidated and hurt by abusive or neglectful parents may either find themselves wanting her crucified or wanting to protect her out of the symbolic fear of getting hurt again, or because of misdirected pity.

By way of an update, Sandra Hart was convicted of her *tenth* drunken driving offense in December 1999—shame on the State of Minnesota for letting it go this long—and was finally sentenced to some jail time in January 2000.

The Grace in South Central L.A.[40]

In 1990, Myrtle Faye Rumph's son was killed in a drive-by shooting. Within hours, friends and relatives had gathered to plan revenge. They watched and waited, put the neighborhood under surveillance, and planned to kill his killers. But Myrtle Faye intervened, stating quietly that she didn't want to avenge her son's death, but rather, she wanted to memorialize his life. With no money and no government assistance, she set up the beginnings of a storefront teen center in his name. It was to be a safe and supportive place for teens to congregate, away from the violence and death that they experienced regularly. When she ran out of money, she sold her house and kept the center going. Five years later, her center had a yearly budget of two hundred thousand dollars, and had 125 teenagers gathering there on a daily basis. She summed it up when she said, ". . . I didn't want to wait around for the city, the county or the state to give me the money to do it. It's up to black people to change our own destiny. That's what I'm trying to do."

As the author in this *L.A. Times* article pointed out, Rumph "had an unlikely manner and scholastic background" for someone who accomplished this. She had to drop out of high school in her junior year to help support her family and later came to Los Angeles as a single mother with five dollars to her name. What a remarkable woman she must be. We have been reading her story to audiences since 1995, and each time we do, we have to hold back the tears to be able to finish reading it. What an awe-inspiring model for us and everyone else. We are especially grateful for a person like her because her wisdom is so profound, and her humility so deep, that we are forced to admit how far we have to go just to come close to her emotional and spiritual competence. Without people like her to remind us of how limited *and* limitless we are, we would certainly be lost. Myrtle Faye Rumph is one of the clearest examples of unmitigated power that we have encountered in the contemporary press. Her life is nothing less than an invitation to improve ourselves. (To learn more, or to help, go to: *www.wootencenter.org.*)

The Little Things

We sometimes forget that the way we choose to interpret the world determines what we'll see. A large piece of how we interpret the world hinges on what we choose to focus on at any given moment. It is a big universe. What will I see when I wake up this morning? You always leave your jacket draped over the edge of the sink in the laundry room when you come home. Will I perceive this as a direct attempt to make my life miserable? As a blatant disregard for my desire for order and neatness? Am I still *that* narcissistic? Or will I see it as simply one of the differences between you and me? And will I love you for those differences, knowing that if you weren't different, we wouldn't be capable of having a relationship at all? When I awake today, will I engage in weeping and the gnashing of teeth because you forgot to take the garbage out last night, or will I focus on the fact that we had a lovely evening together and I am reminded of what a wonderful partner I have, even as I begin to head into the challenges of the day?

A Blessing in County Tipperary

We were working in Ireland a few years ago and were blessed with a beautiful experience. It was something we had experienced over and over before but it was just different enough to make it eternally memorable. At the end of a long day of presenting difficult information about painful families, we did a concluding exercise in which everyone wrote down three little things that they liked—in America it might be things like fine-tipped pens, playing with a puppy, walking on the beach at night with your lover, a good book, a well-organized hard drive on your computer or the sound of a Harley-Davidson roaring down the open road. It is such a simple exercise, and yet over the years we have seen groups of physicians and attorneys, truck drivers and nurses, social workers and business executives weep openly as each man and woman nervously and proudly reads his or her list while everyone else quietly listens.

The things we appreciate say more about us than almost anything else, which is why we ask our audiences to listen respectfully, read their list, and not explain or defend what they share. What we like, want or appreciate needs no defense. No justification is needed. It is who we are. The list is simply a matter of preference. Read the three items on your list and then pass.

When it happens this way—with reverence, attention and care—it is nearly impossible not to be moved to one's depths as each person reads her or his list. It creates a safe but vulnerable atmosphere that allows each human being in the room to be proud of his or her uniqueness while appreciating and connecting with everyone else, which gives each man and woman in the room the chance to briefly experience the magical paradox of simultaneous separateness and togetherness. *I am unique so no one will ever understand me, but I can see myself in your soul so I will never be alone.*

And so around the room they went, each person nervously awaiting her turn to read her list, each person warmly receiving the list of his fellows. We were tired. One of us had been sick for several days and was ready to rest. It was our first visit to Ireland. We had ancestors here. It was a homecoming, but we were working and therefore had to present our material as professionally as we could. We worried about how we would be received because an American speaker the year before had not been well-received. As the long day slowly came to a close with each person reading the items on his list, it appeared that we had connected with an ancestry we had only read about in books; we shared pain and joy with people we worried might not like us, and we formed an intimate bond with a marvelous group of human beings from another country. As the eighty-fifth person read the three items on his list, we felt tears running down our cheeks, and then we looked up and saw tears running down the cheeks of eighty-five people. All of us had been deeply moved by the experience, which turned out to be the perfect ending to a memorable day.

What did members of our Irish audience like? They mentioned things like fine-tipped pens, playing with a puppy, walking along the edge of the sea with a lover, a good book, quietly fishing on a nearby lake, sitting by a warm fire on a chilly night, the smell of fresh coffee brewing in the morning, big puffy clouds, rain, hugs, children, jogging, quaint little shops, a good heated discussion, movies, sailing, a clean house, a down comforter, horses, good friends, sex, French pastries . . . you know, typical little things that make us happy.

One of life's most pleasant experiences can be to share an afternoon walk with a good friend, especially if we have spent the majority of our life being lonely. The smell of fresh air to a man just released from prison can be the closest thing to heaven on Earth. The warmth of the early summer sunlight penetrating one's skin can be euphoric, especially if it comes after a long, cold winter. Sometimes we have to experience the depths of deprivation before we can truly appreciate the important things in life—the little things. One of the deepest joys of being psychologists is that we are often allowed to witness someone's transformation from unappreciative and addictive to appreciative and spiritual. It's not that we should intentionally deprive ourselves or set out to ruin our lives in the hopes that we will someday be able to appreciate life's subtleties. It's just that when we are not medicating ourselves with addictive or compulsive behaviors, life presents us with enough natural pain and deprivation that eventually we can be grateful for the little things that count so much, but only if we grow up.

If It Pleases . . .

Knowing what pleases us is crucial. If you have the opportunity to visit someone who is suffering from untreated depression you may catch a glimpse of what we mean. This person's surroundings will often reflect his mental state. You may notice few pictures on the walls, no flowers or decorations around the house, no expressions of self to be found anywhere. If these things are present, you might notice that the home has not been cared for lately, as if the person living there is from out of town and on business, with little time to make a home out of his house. What we like, what we want and how we express our inner selves in our living spaces are essential aspects of who we are.

In some families, little attention is paid to aesthetics, and even less to the individual desires of each family member. A child wants her room painted a certain color, but her parents don't listen to her wishes. Mom buys five dollars worth of flowers to decorate the table, and Dad explodes as if she'd just purchased the Taj Mahal. In other families, each person's identity and spirit are viewed as gifts from creation that are to be revered and nurtured for the betterment of the whole. When one child likes a different color than the rest, it is accepted and appreciated as an expression of her individual will. Willfulness is seen as a sign of spirit and identity, not as a sign of impudence and defiance. An infant spies a rattle in her crib, and her heart leaps with excitement as she reaches out her tiny hand to grasp it. She isn't just picking up a toy; she is casting her spirit out into the universe so that it can learn and deepen and expand. A man decorates his new apartment and in doing so he expresses, reinforces and clarifies his identity and his spirit. As we learn what pleases us, as we reach out into creation to feel all that is out there, our inner selves deepen and bloom. When we don't know what we like, and when we never experience what pleases us, it is a clear sign that something is hurting inside.

Relationships Are Astonishingly Easy

It is often said that the things we appreciate about each other also contain the seeds of our discontent. A man says that it drives him crazy that his partner is too fussy about their home, but in the next breath he compliments her on what a good housekeeper she is. A woman complains that her partner is too rational but she admires him for his successful law career. Appreciation is a complex act, and it increases in depth and simplicity as *we* deepen.

When working with couples, we ask each of the partners to take a closer look at what they notice about each other, and then we wonder about these things with them. Wonderment is such a wonderful thing. It sounds like such a simple task. I wonder how I feel when I see you struggle so gallantly with that bump in your road. I wonder what it must be like for you. I wonder why *that* struggle is a struggle for you, whereas it is an easy and natural thing for me. I wonder if it is harder for you than I think it is. I wonder if the struggle is making you grow in ways I can't imagine. I wonder what would happen if I let you in on my wondering.

Ah-h-h. There's the rub. I am looking at you and seeing you struggle. But if I share with you my wonderment, then I am exposing my struggles with *you.* Well, it should be much easier to tell you that I admire your struggle than to tell you what makes me *angry* about you. But wait. It isn't. It's just as risky, because *I'm* exposed, either way. Maybe I'll just sit back here at a distance, play it safe and make magnanimous coaching noises, like "I know you can do it," "I know everything will work out for the best" or "Don't worry about it." But what will happen if I say, "I see you struggling with that, and it unnerves me. I don't know what else to say. Your determination moves me in a way I've never felt before"? Well, now it's a different story. We are suddenly both astonished for completely separate and intertwined reasons. *That's* astonishing.

Whenever I expose my vulnerability to another human being there is the risk of getting hurt. It is surely an act of vulnerability to tell him that I love him dearly and would be miserable without him. And if I let her know that her power is unsettling, but I do so from a position of power and love and the *hope* that she loves me in return, and I know that she is free *not* to love me, *then* we have a connection with the magic that defies description.

It is sheer joy for us to hear a man tell his wife that he values her more than anything else in the world, and that he appreciates all that she does, all that she is, how much she graces his life and what a good friend she has become to him. He says he appreciates her extraversion, how she can go out into the world and meet people and make things happen. He appreciates her smile and her sense of humor, her sensitivity to others' feelings, the fact that she will stand up to him and fight when she feels she needs to, and that she is sexy. A woman tells her husband that she appreciates his strength, his know-how and worldliness, his reflective spirit that balances her extraverted one, his depth, his sense of humor—she has always liked that—and his power and his gentleness. She doesn't like weak, passive men, she says, and he's no weak, passive man.

Many couples tell us that, with regularity, one will spontaneously turn to the other and say, "I love you and appreciate you." The other will bask in the comment and then later will spontaneously say the same kind of thing in return. They don't do this because they read it in a book or because they were told to do it in a workshop. They feel it and mean it because they have suffered life's disappointments and have come to accept what life has to offer and because they know how fragile life is and how fleeting a moment can be.

A man told us how he used to belittle people who appreciated things, especially if they were the simple things in life that enrich us so much. He was a bit like Ebenezer Scrooge in that regard. Everything was a humbug. Adults who enjoyed reading the comics in the newspaper on Sunday morning were "humbugful," as were spy novels, dreaming about the future and holding hands while walking through the park. "How embarrassing for them," he would mutter under his breath. "Grown adults holding hands. How corny. Who cares what color car you have?" he would pronounce. "A car is a means of transporting oneself from point A to point B. Just buy the damned thing and let's get out of here," he would mumble in disgust.

And then he began to lose things. First, he lost a good friend who simply couldn't bear to be around all of the negativity and criticism. Then he lost a lung to cancer. Then his mother died, and then his father. Then his wife divorced him because he was so miserable to live with. And then he was almost killed in an automobile accident, and he had to endure a painful and protracted recovery.

Life had brought him not just to his knees but to death's door, and as he stood at the threshold he realized for the first time that there is no discernible difference between life and death—they are the same—and for the first time in his life he was able to appreciate the little things in life. One day, many years later, he was talking about his second marriage and he said with simplicity and sincerity, "This relationship is so good. There are days when I wake up and have to think twice to make sure I'm not in a fantasy. I am so grateful for this person who sleeps next to me every night. I am grateful for our passion, for our fights, for our laughter, tears and for all the trivial, silly little things that we enjoy together. I never could have appreciated these things ten years ago. I finally have a glimpse of what life is really about."

An old man suffers a stroke and spends his last five years of life nearly bedridden after the previous seventy-five of being active, driven and goal-oriented. Is it a cruel trick or a subtle gift that life has brought to him? Punishment for past sins or a sacred opportunity to fill in the hidden corners of his soul that had been overlooked during his busy life? A woman lives with dependency fears all of her life, and then she spends the last five years of her husband's life in the terror that he might die and she might be alone forever. He dies and she grieves, and then she has peace in her life despite the fact that she is alone. She had to experience the one thing she feared the most before she was able to live with dignity.

We have worked with Americans, Mexicans, Canadians, English, Scots, Irish, South Africans, Japanese, Chinese, French, Norwegians, Swedes, Indians, Poles, Russians, Thais, Germans and many more. The list of little things that human beings like goes on . . .

. . . the crunch of snow beneath your boots on a freezing, moonlit night, flannel underwear, hummingbirds, Chardonnay, Paris at night, the Kohala Coast of Hawaii, dry desert air, the Dave Matthews Band, a wild summer thunderstorm, mountain streams, lots of fresh ground pepper on my salad, a child's laughter, swimming in icy water, my cat, clean teeth, just the right makeup, sensual sex on a warm afternoon, a good play, Bangkok, soft skin, chocolate, Persian rugs, the London Times *on Sunday morning, Labrador retrievers, hardwood floors, fresh sheets, oranges, a symphony orchestra, the desert sunrise, parrots, Mecca, dim sum, glaciers . . .*

14

Manage Your Fear, Hurt, Shame and Loneliness

I feel the same way about solitude as some people
feel about the blessing of the church. It's the light
of grace for me. Never do I close the door behind
me without being conscious that I am carrying out
an act of charity towards myself.

—Peter Hoeg
Miss Smilla's Feeling for Snow

Shame and Hurt in the Front Yard

You are outside shoveling the snow off the stone walkway
leading up to your home. Your husband has just opened the

garage door and is rolling the trash can out to the curb for the weekly pickup. As he turns and walks back toward the house he sees you there, and suddenly he feels a wave of anxiety sweep over him. He approaches you hurriedly and says in a mixed bark and whine, "Why don't you toss the snow over there?" as he points a commanding finger at a spot between the low-growing evergreens and the sugar maple you planted five years ago. "If you pile it where you're piling it now, you're gonna smother those evergreens!"

As if a syringe of pure adrenaline has been shot directly into your aorta, your blood pressure skyrockets, your heart races, your breathing quickens and you feel a rage in your belly the likes of which you've never felt before. You wheel around and face him with fire in your eyes and shout, "Why don't you shut the f--- up!" *I never* swear, you tell yourself, horrified. You glare at him as he shrinks before your very eyes and then sheepishly skulks back into the house.

Fear and Loneliness in the Dining Room

You and your wife are having dinner together on a quiet Thursday evening. The week is almost over, and it's been a long one. And tougher than usual. Neither one of you is in top form, and you're enjoying being with each other without major distractions for the first time all week. You're peacefully discussing plans for the weekend. Suddenly, you remember that you promised one of your good friends that you and your wife would go to the opening of the play he is in at the local community theater. The opening is tomorrow night. You genuinely forgot, and you're hoping beyond hope that your wife will look up, smile excitedly and say, "Oh, great! I'm so glad we get to go! I'm so excited for him!" But she's not likely to say that. You know her better than that.

In the first place, she's an introvert, and so she recharges her batteries by puttering around the house by herself, not by going out and mixing with crowds of people. Second, you both just shared with each other how tired you are and how you are looking forward to a quiet weekend together. Third, as an extravert who has developed his introverted side pretty well, when you heard the words leaving your mouth, a wiser part of you was saying, *You should have said "Damn! I just remembered I promised Bob that I'd go to his opening tomorrow night. Would you be okay if I just went and came right back after the play is over?"* But the part of you that wants to try to make everybody happy held sway, and now the words were out and the tension was in the air.

"You what?" she began, angrily. "What the hell were you *thinking?* I am *exhausted!*" She stood up from the table, whirled around, and as she stormed out of the dining room she yelled back, "You are *so* inconsiderate! I can't believe you!" You become engulfed by anxiety as you hear the bedroom door slam. Because you're tired, you can't soothe yourself. The fear gets bigger. It feels like the marriage is suddenly over. The gulf between the two of you is unbearable. Instead of settling yourself down, which would give her some room to do the same, you head upstairs to the bedroom. The door is locked. Your fear gets bigger. You've flooded.

You pound on the door and in desperation try to reason with her in a voice you hope is loud enough to pass through the door. She yells, "Stop yelling! Just go away! I just need some space!" Well, to a person who is on the verge of emotionally flooding, the phrase "I just need some space" is code for "I am locked in here because I am about to pick up the phone and call my associate from work who is divorced and who talks all the time about how much fun she's having dating and having sex with all these exciting new men she's found." You finally slip across the boundary between upset and flooded.

"Open this door *right now! I mean it! OPEN IT!!*" You pound harder and harder until the door jamb starts to split.

"That's it! I'm out of here!" she screams.

The Feelings Beneath the Rage

Let's stop here and catch our breath. Scenes like the two above are played out all across the country in homes peopled by doctors and lawyers and plumbers and bricklayers and drug dealers and prostitutes and schoolteachers and psychologists and everyone in between. They demonstrate two critical facts:

1. Violence and rage occur as a reaction to our fear, hurt, shame, loneliness or some combination of the four, and . . .

2. When we are violent or rageful, it is not because of something the other person does, but because of something *we* do *not* do.

For this reason, this may be the most important chapter in the book for many people. *Fear, hurt, shame* and *loneliness* are pivotal emotions because they are involved in both the deepest connections between partners as well as the most damaging wounds inflicted by partners on each other. As with so many other things in human affairs, there is a powerful paradox surrounding these primal emotions. It is said that the deepest, most penetrating intimacy between people occurs at the level of their vulnerability. We have also said the same thing in our statement that "the deepest experience of intimacy takes place at the level of our weakness."

Being Vulnerable vs. Being Out of Control

But that's a very qualified statement, because in order to have truly deep intimacy at the level of our weakness, a person must be very strong. Strength, of course, is the ability to experience our emotions while keeping them relatively well-contained so that they do not spill over and flood everyone around us. Thus we note the profound difference between being with someone who is shedding tears deeply, sobbing with gut-wrenching grief, but who we know is able to contain himself, versus being with one who cries uncontrollably but leaves us with the fear that at any moment he will go off the deep end. The problem in trying to explain this, especially in a media "sound bite," is that on the surface the two instances look exactly alike, especially to someone who lacks emotional intelligence.

"When she'd come up and sit by me, I felt myself recoiling inside. I just assumed it was because I was a guy—you know, guys aren't supposed to be comfortable with feelings—but it *wasn't* because I was a guy. It was because she had no boundaries inside of herself. It was like her intestines were spilling out into my lap and onto the floor, and I was supposed to sit there calmly and take it all in, or be accused of lacking the ability to be intimate! Good God! I am so glad I talked to a therapist about this. It *was* me, but not in the way I first thought. It was me doubting my own perceptions."

The more at ease we become with the beauty of the complex parts of ourselves, the more distinct is the line between what that man just described, and what this next man described. "We were having breakfast one Saturday morning, and I started reading an article to her from the newspaper. It was an emotional story, and my lip started to quiver as I took a breath and looked up at her for a second. Her eyes had begun to well up with tears. I stopped. She started to speak, and her voice cracked as the tears trickled down her cheeks. 'My father was so cruel,' she began. 'I don't know what was wrong with him. And my mother to this day has never acknowledged it. When I was a little girl he made nasty, snide remarks to me for no reason. I was a sweet little girl trying to be good all the time. He said, "You think you're so smart. Well, *I* know better." I looked up in my mother's eyes hoping for something, anything, some acknowledgment that what he said was wrong, and she just looked down at the potatoes she was peeling and said, "Come over here and help me. I always have too much work to do."'"

This man continued. "One of the things that I admire and appreciate so much about her is how she can do that. In all our years together, I have never felt smothered or engulfed by her feelings, and yet she is remarkably open without being out of control. Vulnerable without being needy. I have learned so much from her. She is such a gift."

The Difference Between "Having a Breakdown" and Having Our Feelings

To understand what we are trying to get across here, you must realize that quite a few people would describe the women in both stories above as "having a breakdown." If it weren't so confusing for him, it would almost be comical to hear a man say that "I almost had a breakdown during our sales meeting when that S.O.B. singled me out and started blaming me for the company's poor third-quarter performance. The two V.P.s and the entire sales force were at that meeting. Despite the fact that my sales exceeded everyone else's, I felt two inches tall!"

"You almost had a breakdown?" we asked.

"Yes. I could feel my lip start to quiver, and it was all I could do to keep my emotions in check."

"What happened next?"

"I composed myself and then I said, 'My sales figures are the best of the entire team. I think we can recover our performance if we look at what's really going on in the marketplace.'"

We thought, *What a great way to handle it!* And then we asked, looking just puzzled enough not to be sarcastic, "So, where was the near-breakdown?"

"You know. I almost cried."

In Other Words

Fear, hurt, shame and loneliness are normal, healthy emotions. They are also very powerful emotions. When they are not contained, or when they aren't identified and acknowledged, they can lead to rage and violence or to extreme manipulation and smothering. When they are integrated and contained, they lead to the deepest levels of intimacy imaginable. People who get confused by this (1) have a hard time separating their own reactions from the reactions of others, and (2) tend to clump all emotional reactions into one category, getting flooded by even the healthy emotions of themselves and others, and/or not being able to distinguish between emotions that are "over the top" and emotions that are expressed with integrity and grace.

Important "Feelings Facts"

When looking at our Front Yard and Dining Room examples, Daniel Goleman[41] might say that these people's brains were being *emotionally hijacked.* John Gottman[42] would probably call them instances of *emotional flooding.* Dr. Redford Williams of Duke University, author of *Anger Kills,*[43] might be concerned about these people's elevated cortisol levels creating lesions inside their coronary arteries. Whatever you call it, it isn't good for you and it isn't good for the relationship. In years of research with couples, Gottman has shown that any interchange occurring after you're flooded is going to be damaging to the relationship. Really great couples have ways to *soothe* themselves and each other so that the frequency and intensity of these incidents are minimized. But some people don't even know what is happening to them before, during or even after scenes like these.

Biology and psychology students learn that emotions are centered in the limbic system of the brain, which is sometimes referred to as the *reptilian brain* because it's as complex as a reptile's brain gets—its brain is designed to react quickly to its environment, and that's pretty much it. For a very well-written, comprehensive explanation of how this all works, get a copy of Goleman's *Emotional Intelligence* and study the section on the brain and emotions. It is fascinating.

In a nutshell, a stimulus event happens—seeing a rattle-snake coiled up and ready to strike five feet in front of you, having your husband criticize the hard work you are doing or believing that your wife is about to leave you—and then a rapid-fire sequence follows. Information hurtles back to the visual or auditory cortex of the brain so that you can see or hear what is happening, it then radiates back and down to the limbic system where you "feel" something about the information—fear or shame, for example—and then it radiates up into the cerebral cortex, the higher part of the brain that allows you to think, unlike a snake. We think, and then, hopefully, we temper our reaction to better fit the situation. Goleman pointed out one intriguing additional element in the sequence, which is that a small portion of the stimulus event goes *directly* to the limbic system, which means that we react to the rattlesnake—to use Goleman's example—a split-second before we actually "see" it! The upshot of all this is that:

- We respond very quickly to what is going on around us.

- We're going to feel what we feel whether we think so or not.

- In most cases, we *Homo Sapiens* have the great good fortune to be able to *choose* how we respond because we have a neocortex in addition to a limbic system.

- People can get into trouble because they aren't aware of their feelings, or because they are too aware of them.

- Feelings are expressed nonverbally, so the words are almost irrelevant.

- While they are registered in the brain, they are felt in the body.

- They are going on all the time, which means when you say, "I'm not feeling anything right now," we know that you must mean you aren't *aware* of what you're feeling right now.

Fear, Hurt, Shame and Loneliness Are Good Emotions: Unless They're over the Top

Fear

Fear gives us wisdom. Being completely fearless means doing dumb things. Being courageous means doing scary things because they must be done, but knowing how scared we are when we do them. Watch the opening minutes of

Saving Private Ryan and this will be clear. If you pretend you have no fear because it was shamed and belittled when you were younger or because no one in your family acknowledged their fear in front of you, then you will continue to burn your hand on the same stove or get hurt in the same kind of relationship, over and over again, or act out your fear with anger or rage.

When I (JCF) was a child, I collected snakes as a hobby. My little friend and I were chasing a rare lizard up a gully, and we were so excited that we forgot where we were and what we were doing. The lizard darted under a big boulder in the middle of the ravine, and as we reached under the boulder for the lizard, we heard the blood-chilling buzz of a rattlesnake that struck out at us just as we leaped to the side and out of its range. As first-graders, we would have been dead had it bitten us. From that day forward—right up till now, forty-nine years later—whenever I hike those dry coastal mountains where I spent my youth, I have just enough anxiety to make sure that I don't do something stupid that I'll regret for the rest of my (perhaps short) life. I also like to add at this point in the story that as a good adult child of an alcoholic family, it took me several decades longer to safely begin avoiding the human rattlesnakes in my life.

Pain/Hurt

This warns us when we have been damaged, or when we are about to sustain damage, and so this is also crucial for emotional and physical health. In families where pain is ignored, denied, minimized or belittled, children lose the information that is often critical for one's survival. For example, if you minimize how painful an abusive relationship is and make excuses for horrible treatment from another, your life may be in danger. If you grow up in what we call a "pain denial family system," you may have a difficult time realizing how and why you keep getting into really painful situations, and you won't have the crucial feedback that you need in order to extricate yourself from the pain. If your hand is burning on a hot stove but you're in denial of your physical pain, you'll probably leave your hand there until it has third-degree burns on it. Pain is good. It helps us avoid further damage.

Shame

Shame lets us be accountable, accountability lets us have humility, humility helps us to be spiritual and spirituality allows us to have healthy power. One definition of a perpetrator is someone who is shameless. Having high self-esteem does not mean that we have no shame. It means we have *appropriate* shame. Shame is the feeling that we are flawed—that we have defects—and all human beings have defects. So all human beings feel some shame from time to time. When we can be embarrassed about those defects, we can change them. "I keep making sarcastic comments to people, thinking that it's cute or funny. But Joe Smith called me on it in front of everyone the other day, and I was really embarrassed. It hurt, too. At first I was really angry at Joe and wanted to lash out and get even, but now that I've thought about it for awhile, I think it's me who needs to change, not him. He was right." *That* is an example of healthy shame in action.

Psychologist Gershen Kaufman[44] wrote that shame is the denial of our right to depend on others, and so it has a lot to do with being "cut out of the herd," and with feeling "different." When you are singled out as either *worse than others,* or *better than everyone else,* you will often feel shame. Obviously, it will manifest itself differently if you're constantly told that you're better than everyone else. In that case, you'll probably become arrogant, snooty, spoiled and narcissistic, which is the antithesis of humility and true power. *One of the most powerful ways to shame someone is to ignore her.* This is why people often react so violently or so deeply when ignored by someone important to them. This is why being passive-aggressive is so destructive.

Loneliness

Loneliness is a very uncomfortable feeling, which causes many people to ask how this could be a positive emotion. Because like wolves and apes, we are social animals who by being social have been able to survive on the planet longer than if we were roaming the planet alone, foraging for food, isolated from one another. The discomfort of loneliness propels us into groups, and we survive. Recent research shows that people with a good support system also live longer and fight serious disease much better than people who are emotionally isolated from others. If you're interested, read University of California San Francisco Medical Center cardiologist Dean Ornish's book, *Love and Survival*.[45] In it, he cites most of the major studies that show the powerful role of our relationships in our physical health.

If we lack the unconscious rules that would make having complex relationships possible, then we will eventually create a shell around ourselves so that we won't keep getting hurt. Unfortunately, the shell we create is the very thing that prevents further relationships, and so we become even more lonely and isolated. A negative spiral begins, and then we get stuck. To get out of this trap, we need to admit how lonely we are and then recognize that the loneliness is actually more harmful and painful than would be the hurt that comes from trying to make our relationships work.

Soothing Yourself

In *The Search for the Real Self: Unmasking the Personality Disorders of Our Age*,[46] psychiatrist James Masterson created a universal, timeless list he called "The Capacities of the Real Self." These capacities are what distinguish a mature, intact, integrated person from a less fully developed, perhaps wounded, person. They include "the ability to experience a wide range of feelings deeply," the "ability to be alone" and the *"ability to soothe painful feelings."* The lack of this ability to soothe one's feelings is implicated in a wide range of mental health problems, but nowhere is its presence as obvious than in addictions and disorders of impulse control, especially rage problems.

When a wife goes into a rage and hurls a crystal goblet at her husband, it is because she is unable to soothe herself.

When a husband gets so hurt by his wife's criticism of him that he stubbornly refuses to interact with her for days, and when his hurt is just as "big" three days later as it was when she first made the critical remark, it is often a self-soothing problem.

The ability to soothe oneself has both biological as well as behavioral roots. In the early 1970s, in psychology graduate programs, the newly emerging field of newborn infant physiology was taking shape. We learned that there are often vast individual differences in infants' reactivity to stimulation—some infants remain calm and unflappable while others startle and cry when presented with the identical stimulus. Some seem to soothe themselves automatically, while others require a great deal of help from their parents.

By the time a person is an adult, it is hard to determine how much of this "soothing capacity" is learned and how much is physiological. We know that if you were traumatized repeatedly as a child, or if you suffered a massive single trauma, you *might* develop post-traumatic stress disorder (PTSD), the symptoms of which are now familiar to many people. Overreactivity to stimuli that parallel the original trauma, emotional numbing, powerful flashbacks, depression and a generalized increase in emotional arousal are a few of these symptoms. What we now know is that traumas like these can actually alter the neurochemistry of the brain, so that the change becomes relatively persistent. That is why certain medications have been shown to be helpful with PTSD.

It is also important to know that clinical depression can

act as a magnifying glass for uncomfortable feelings such as anxiety, sadness, shame and hurt; and that in some cases, people who have intractable rage problems are helped immensely by one of the selective serotonin reuptake inhibitors (SSRIs) like Prozac or Celexa.

But make no mistake about it: A man who beats up his girlfriend or runs another car off the road in a fit of rage is not necessarily suffering from PTSD or clinical depression. In fact, we suspect that a large number of these people are not. You could just as well create a person who fails to soothe her feelings by babying and spoiling her as she grows up, by exposing her to role models who display little impulse control or by constantly intruding past her age-appropriate boundaries as she is growing up, to name just a few.

Soothing Strategies

Physical Health

By far, the most common emotions involved in problems between people are shame and fear of abandonment, as demonstrated in the first two examples in this chapter. We are most likely to "lose it" when we feel under psychological attack or when we fear the loss of important relationships. So what can be done?

If you are having problems calming yourself or managing your feelings, we urge you to look first at your physical health, which includes your neurophysiology and your diet.

People can be irritable because of a shortage of serotonin, hormonal imbalances, dietary deficiencies or metabolic disorders such as hyperthyroidism. You may have trouble soothing yourself if you drink too much coffee or if you have high blood pressure. Certain herbal supplements can cause all sorts of problems, including fatigue and memory difficulties. Ginseng can cause high blood pressure and nervousness in some people. We mention these first because they are often the last thing that people look at in diagnosing emotional problems, and it would save a lot of pain and heartache if they were the first.

How You Think

Thirteen years ago we wrote a book chapter entitled "You Are What You Think (Sometimes)." Therapists who help their clients use cognitive behavior therapy (CBT) methods, and the researchers who developed these techniques know that the general way in which we view the world has a tremendous impact on how we handle our feelings. It has recently been demonstrated that doing cognitive behavioral training with people who have severe obsessive compulsive disorder (OCD) can not only help them begin to manage their obsessing and repetitive behaviors by managing how they think, but when they do, their brain activity changes just like it would if they were being treated for the problem with medication! In other words, our brain chemistry affects how we think, but in some cases, how we think can also alter our brain chemistry.

Martin Seligman, past president of the American

Psychological Association and author of the bestselling *Learned Optimism,*[47] is one of many experts who have made cognitive behavioral therapy available to the general public in a very user-friendly form. He shows his readers how to correct the kinds of negative thinking that keep many people stuck in the victim role indefinitely. For some people, adversity is quickly framed as a challenge to be faced and eventually overcome, even if overcoming the adversity means accepting tragic loss and moving on to a new life. For others, adversity is quickly interpreted as further proof that "life's a bitch and then you die."

Many clients over the years have told us that events they are able to handle quite well in the present would have thrown them into an irreversible tailspin a few years earlier. They attribute much of the difference to changes in the way they think about the world. "Life's a bitch and then you die" is one way to look at an imperfect world in which painful and unfair things happen to everybody, and if you're wearing just the right pair of lenses, the world fits it perfectly. Of course, what we see is often what we get. My lenses will actually help me create the kind of miserable life with which I am so unhappy. If every twist or turn in the road is met by my whines of misery, then, of course, the only people who will tolerate being around me are either other victims like myself, or perpetrators. Either way, they'll make my life even more miserable.

But if I put on a different set of lenses—voilà!—"Life's a bitch and then you die" becomes "Life is a wondrous mystery filled with routine annoyances, frustrations, tragedy, unbearable misery, rapturous joy and the endless excitement that comes with getting up each day, meeting the people we meet, loving those we love—and getting angry at them— and continuing to grow and deepen right up until the day we die." It's the difference between having and not having trust and hope in the face of seemingly hopeless situations, which leads to the next source of soothing.

Connections with Others

Because we human beings are the ultimate social animals, our "disconnections" from each other are prime sources of intense distress. By the same token, *healthy connections with others are the primary source of trust and hope.* In summarizing a large-scale study of adults who experienced significant trauma in childhood, distinguished developmental psychologist Uri Bronfenbrenner of Cornell University found that only one thing separated those who eventually "made it" psychologically from those who didn't—having at least one person in your life when you were a child who was "just plain crazy about you."

As we have mentioned before, having truly intimate relationships increases our resistance to all sorts of problems, including physical illnesses. Dean Ornish noted that there is a new field called "psychoneuroimmunology"—the study of the effects of social factors on the immune system of animals. In discussing what psychologists call the theory of "object relations," he noted that:

> *. . . people often develop patterns of relating as adults that are not so different from how they learned to relate as children. If you grew up in a family in which love, nurturing,*

and intimacy are in short supply, then you are more likely to view your current relationships with mistrust and suspicion.[48]

Of course, the reverse is also true. If you grew up with healthy love from your family, then you are more likely to be "open and trusting in your ongoing relationships." He goes on to list several studies which point to the phenomenal fact that *it is a greater physical health risk to not have good, solid, intimate support in your life than it is to smoke cigarettes!*

The upshot of all this is that one of the most important "soothing agents" a human being can employ is the support and friendship of other human beings. For men, it is especially important that a good chunk of this support come from nonsexual, nonromantic relationships, because putting all of one's need for intimacy into the romantic type of relationship can be both risky and additionally stressful.

Before we close this chapter, remember that most people in the United States die of diseases of lifestyle—lack of exercise, poor diet, smoking, alcohol and drugs, stress, and above all, lack of true emotional support. These are all risk factors that increase stress. Learning to reduce these risk factors not only increases your life span, but it also soothes you. And soothing yourself in healthy ways means that you will one day be able to have a really great relationship!

15

Own Your Own Part

God, grant me the serenity to accept
the people I cannot change,
the courage to change the person I can,
and the wisdom to know it's me.

—Anonymous

You're Always . . .

Picture the following scenario: Your husband is pretty much late all the time. The two of you have never missed a flight, but you have come hair-raisingly close so many times that the walls of your stomach are nearly eroded from the excess acid. You have sat down at your opera seats twenty minutes into it so many times that years ago you stopped visualizing yourself calmly waiting for the curtain to rise. You have been forced to wait outside in the lobby of the theater and watch the play on black-and-white closed-circuit television until the end of Act One so many times that you trigger knowing and sympathetic smiles from the ushers, who you are convinced joke about the two of you when you're out of view.

You have been married for ten years, and for ten years you have been seen speeding down the freeway, screaming at each other, hands flailing about in confused gestures of anger and hurt, or sitting in a cold, icy silence that is so intense that there appears to be a force field surrounding your car. You think you know that other couples struggle with this issue of "being on time vs. being late," but it is hard for you to imagine that anyone else in the world has it as bad as you. You have tried "everything in the book," including the extreme measure of leaving without him a few times, but there has been little movement in a long, painful decade.

What makes it so bad, you have noticed, is that you feel so . . . so . . . so betrayed when he does this. You feel like he's doing it on purpose to punish you, that if he loved you, which he must not, he'd recognize how much it drives you crazy, and then he'd change. Surely he can detect the anxiety in your voice and on your face. Surely the level of your anger tells him how important this is to you. He must hate you deep down inside. *He must feel contemptuous,* you tell yourself. What makes it even harder is that you adore him and are convinced that he is the best thing that has ever happened to you.

Today you find yourself sitting in the car in the parking lot in front of his office, waiting for him to emerge. The two of you are going to the early movie on Thursday evening to avoid the weekend crowds. A thousand images flash through your brain as a thousand pulses of chaotic energy pulse through your body. You feel your body "revving up" for another routine, awful, gut-wrenching confrontation.

And then something happens. You gently shift the focus of your mind's eye toward a picture of your husband as the hard-working, responsible provider that he is, as the excellent father that he is, as the marvelous lover that he is, and as the human being who has a vulnerable side just like you and everyone else in the world. You imagine what he must be doing in there, how he must be feeling. You see him rushing around, dictating one more brief letter, signing one more contract so he can drop it in the mail on the way to the movie, returning the last phone call of the day so he can devote his full attention to your evening together.

Within seconds, your heart rate, blood pressure and brain-wave activity decrease to acceptable levels. In a few more seconds, they decrease some more, and the peripheral blood vessels in your hands and feet and limbs relax and open up, filling you with a relaxed, warm feeling all over. Twenty minutes after the appointed hour, you see him coming through the double glass doors of the tasteful office complex, with a fairly good attempt to maintain a cheerful expression on his face, but not quite good enough to mask the deep anxiety that he feels. He jumps in the car and gives you a peck on the cheek as he says, "I'm really sorry I'm late. I had to finish up this contract so I could mail it on the way to the movie."

With your body still feeling the warmth despite the part of your consciousness that is trying to rev up for another confrontation, you reach over to him and firmly, affectionately, and pausing for the slightest of moments to emphasize how sincere you are, you rest your hand on his forearm and say, "Sometimes I forget to tell you how much I admire how successful you are at your career, and how hard you work to provide for me and the kids." His lip starts to quiver and his eyes get misty and then your eyes get misty. He melts. You melt. The rest of the evening is pure magic.

The Mother from . . .

We have worked with several grown women who had these sorts of issues with their mothers. The most dramatic case was a woman in her mid-forties who was very competent, with huge responsibilities at her job. She started therapy with us "to clear up some relationship problems" with her mother, and in the course of taking her history, it was apparent that her seventy-year-old mother wielded tremendous power over all four of the grown children. Our client reported that no one in the family had *ever* taken on Mom, because her secret weapon was that she could go for months without speaking to family members if she felt they needed to be "punished." It's the absolute power of love-withdrawal, one of the cruelest ways a person can gain power in a family.

A couple of years prior to contacting us, our client had taken assertiveness training classes at the corporation where she was an executive. After several weeks of practice, her assertiveness coach said that she was ready to give it a go. The problem was that whenever she and her mother were together, Mom would rifle through her daughter's purse as if it was her own. She would even comment on the contents, suggest that her daughter might want to clean it out now and then, and so forth. Needless to say, our client felt invaded, belittled, ashamed and angry.

So, armed with her new techniques, she had met her mother for lunch one day and intentionally left her purse on the seat when she got up to make a phone call. When she returned, her mother was snooping through her purse again. She took a deep breath, composed herself and then began, "Mother, I need to tell you something." Her mother stopped for a moment and looked up. "Mother, I feel invaded when you go through my purse like that. I would like you to stop doing it."

Her mother looked mildly surprised as she said, defensively, "Oh, pooh, dear. Are you making a mountain out of a molehill again? You know I just have your best interests at heart."

Our client replied, "Nevertheless, I really don't want you to go through my purse. It makes me very angry."

"Well, I think we should just change the subject, dear. It's getting way too hot in here right now," her mother answered, in a very maternalistic tone.

And that was that. Our client heard a few days later from her sister, who reported that their mother was so upset she thought she might be on the verge of a heart attack, and that she'd been having crying jags for the past several days!

Our client said that this was the way it always went, which was why no one ever wanted to confront Mother directly— her shame and the defenses that followed, including the emotional tantrums, weren't worth it. Her mother hadn't spoken to her for four months after this incident, which had left our client feeling abandoned, ashamed, helpless and angry.

She joined one of our women's therapy groups where for the first time in her life, she told us, she was experiencing what it must be like to be a member of a healthy family. People listened to each other, avoided giving a lot of advice, laughed and cried together, all under relatively safe conditions because there was someone who was in charge, but who wasn't authoritarian or manipulative. After a few months in group, she felt genuinely connected enough to make another effort with her mother. The key for her was going to be to use the power of her own love for her mother, and to assume the best about her mother—that in some distorted way, her mother really *did* have her daughter's best interests at heart when she went through her purse.

Human beings always behave a certain way for a reason, even if the behavior isn't the healthiest in the world. Our client was to assume that her mother wanted to be loved and respected just as much as the next person, and that like with a child having tantrums, if someone could gain the upper hand with her without making it look or feel like a direct confrontation, she would respond well. So we helped this woman practice being the respectful, powerful, grown-up woman that she was at work, but now in relationship with her mother. This meant simply refining her earlier attempt at being assertive and making sure to add a strong piece of affirmation for her mother as she gently removed the purse from the center of their relationship.

She practiced and practiced and got support from the group and shared her fears about it blowing up and resulting in a six-month alienation from her mother, and then she said she was ready. She invited her mother over for lunch, and while she was making sandwiches at the side counter in the kitchen, she looked around and noticed her mother facing the built-in desktop on the other side of the center island. Her mother was going through her purse!

She noticed what she was feeling, composed herself, and then in one smooth, uninterrupted, fluid maneuver, she brightly and warmly glided around the center island toward the wall where the desktop was, gently but deliberately removed the purse from her mother's hands all the while saying very cheerfully, and without an iota of snippiness or cattiness in her voice, "Oh, Mother, I stopped letting people go through my purse a long time ago. . . ." As she said that, she glided right around to the cabinet in the opposite wall and put it up on one of the higher shelves, and without any disruption in the flow of her movements or conversation, she moved next to her mother, put her arm around her and continued, ". . . and you're the greatest mom in the world, and I love you. Let's have a nice lunch together."

And that was the end of the problem. Her mother nearly melted right there on the kitchen floor because her daughter had so deftly done two things at the same time: (1) unequivocally blocked her mother's intrusion into her purse and (2) unequivocally affirmed the lovability and goodness of a seventy-year-old woman who had never once been affirmed in a way that could get past her very rational defenses that were installed when she was a little girl growing up with parents who were tired, overworked Scandinavian farmers who believed that outward signs of affection were inappropriate. Our client came to group the next week with the composure and self-possession that could only be present in a grown-up woman.

The Balancing Act

Jim Maddock[49] says that when a couple comes to him for divorce counseling, he tells them that they will be successful in the process if, after the divorce is finalized and they are on their own, the only question that each asks himself or herself is this: *"What did I do to contribute to the failure of this marriage?"* For most people, divorce is a painful and frightening process that taps into the most primitive recesses of the psyche. Consequently, the need to defend our ego is as strong or stronger than our need to defend what we believe we are entitled to in a divorce settlement. Dr. Maddock's challenge is therefore a formidable one. If that challenge is accepted, both parties will benefit immeasurably.

David Schnarch bases his successful marital-sexual therapy model not on sexual technique or behavior like earlier models, but on the concept of *psychological differentiation.* He wrote that:

Well-differentiated people can agree without feeling like they're "losing themselves," and can disagree without feeling alienated and embittered. They can stay connected with people who disagree with them and still "know who they are." They don't have to leave the situation to hold onto their sense of self.[50]

We, too, advocate that you take the focus off your partner and instead put it where it will actually have an effect—maintaining your identity. In our 1988 book, *Adult Children: The Secrets of Dysfunctional Families,* we defined intimacy as *the ability to be in relationship with someone without sacrificing our identity in the process.*[51] This ability to maintain who we are while still maintaining closeness with another is no small feat. On one side of the coin, it is pretty easy to protect who you are by the strategy of not being in the relationship, but then the relationship suffers. That is why two of Gottman's Four Horsemen are defensiveness and withdrawal. Both of these strategies for maintaining one's identity are effective, but they keep us away from the other person and can be used to manipulate in incredibly powerful ways. And, if employed regularly, they prevent us from having a truly healthy identity anyway.

On the other side of the coin, it is pretty easy to sacrifice your identity for the sake of the relationship, but then what kind of relationship can it be? If, as Rilke wrote, "Love is two solitudes that touch and greet and protect each other," then how can it be love? If I lose myself in you, then there is no "me" left, which means there is no "me" for you to have a relationship with, which means there is no relationship! The balancing act, as implied by Schnarch's quote and ours, above, is to maintain ourself while simultaneously maintaining the relationship, and to do so honorably, which is where the crucial question of personal accountability comes into play.

Personal Accountability

A woman is miserable in her marriage and then suddenly finds she is falling in love with another man. She is so lonely and empty in her marriage and so afraid of disturbing the painful balance between her, her husband and her children that she convinces herself to accept the affair as the lesser of two evils—divorce being the other. As she gets more deeply embroiled in the affair, it becomes harder and harder to juggle both relationships until one day the whole delicately balanced house of cards comes crashing down around her. She looks into the frightened eyes of her husband who has just asked her point-blank if she is having an affair, and as she says "yes" she realizes that the greatest damage that she has done to him is to lie when she knew that he suspected something all along, because it deprived him of the dignity of being able to respond to reality rather than a fabrication.

We all weave tangled webs within the structure of our lives now and then. Many people fall into extramarital affairs without seeming to know how it happened. The critical question is, "How do we handle our relationship pain in the future once we have seen and felt the terrible damage caused by this kind of deceit?" A woman who is open to the deepening of integrity and honor within herself will take the huge risk to do a personal accounting of the experience. Her first action after doing this might be to apologize, without excuses, for interfering with her husband's reality and therefore his dignity. She might wait patiently as he expresses his shock, his outrage, his deep hurt and betrayal and his fears. Owning up to the affair levels the playing field just as keeping it secret gives her more power than is fair. Once it is out in the open, she might also act honorably by either ending the marriage if she feels it is hopeless, or by ending the affair so that she can work on the marriage and give it another chance, unfettered by the intrusion of the other relationship.

Regardless of what happens to her marriage, if this woman is becoming truly accountable and honorable, she will no longer be free to choose a hidden affair as an indirect way of dealing with relationship pain in the future. It simply won't be an option any longer because she knows from firsthand experience how much destruction it causes.

As our clients move towards accountability, we liken the experience to being in a room with doors in each corner, and then painting themselves into the corner of their own choosing. If it is an accountable choice, they will paint themselves into the corner where the door opens up to honesty and directness in relationships so that their only available choice will be to resolve the disappointment and unhappiness in their current relationship, cleanly and respectfully, before considering moving on to another relationship.

An *adult* man, in this case, can weather the end of even the deepest of relationships because he knows that life is filled with endings. It is the lack of consistency, honesty and integrity that makes him feel so crazy. And it is the lack of accountability that keeps him stuck in the old, painful relationship. A grown-up man can come to accept that his relationship is over if his partner is forthright and clear about what is in her heart. When she maintains her false dignity by not being honest, then he must struggle with the disrespect implied by her lack of honesty—a struggle that is harder to release.

Accountability does not mean that we continually beat ourselves up for all of our limitations. As therapists, we help people see that their defenses, manipulations, addictions and self-defeating behaviors developed as a way to protect themselves from painful circumstances when they were children, and that as children they did not have the power to protect themselves in healthy ways. This allows the person to have self-acceptance and forgiveness so that he can work through the shame of his limitations. Yet, as Oregon and Southern California therapist Lyndel Brennan notes:

> *Acceptance of our own or another's limitations does not mean that we condone those limitations. We can accept ourselves, "warts and all," but we must also be ready to grow and overcome our limitations as we become able. We can forgive another's hurting us, but we can also expect him to work on his problems so that he stops the hurt.*[52]

Cultivating Integrity, Honor and Accountability

Jean Piaget[53] said that children learn more about empathy while playing in the sandbox than from being told to memorize rules. As we struggle with each other, we directly experience the impact of our behavior on others, and theirs on us. I take your toy away from you and laugh at your tears, and then a bigger or faster child takes my toy away from me and I cry. I lie about my commitment to you, and it violates your trust; then another person lies about his commitment to me, and it violates my trust. These experiences can then allow us to no longer behave respectfully just because the rules say we must, but because of our deepened empathy and understanding of the reasons underlying the rules.

Does this mean that I must kill someone before I can understand why killing is wrong? Of course not. Life experiences are generalizable, and the human mind is perfectly capable of extrapolating from a less severe example to a more severe one. If someone beats me with words and attempts to kill my spirit with emotional neglect, can I not get a strong feeling for what it must be like to be beaten with a bat and to have my life taken from me?

We believe that each human being, no matter how much he hurts later, is born with an empathic/ethical drive. This may sound like a pipe dream given the violence in our society today, but we don't think so. We have seen what appeared to be incorrigible offenders eventually reclaim their dignity by becoming accountable. We have worked with people so driven by their compulsive sexuality that they never thought they could maintain a sexually monogamous relationship with their partner. We have also seen them become monogamous because they were able to heal and then choose accountability over betrayal.

Accountability is a choice. It is an attribute of the soul that can be cultivated. And while being accountable means that we lose certain "freedoms," it also means that we gain immeasurable gifts along the way, which is why it is worth pursuing.

It is essential to respect the truth that integrity, honor and accountability begin in our homes and then spread past those four walls into the world beyond. A little boy overhears his mother say to his father, "You hurt my feelings when you said that, and I didn't like it." Then he hears his father say, "You're right. I'm sorry. I was out of line with that comment." Day in and day out, year after year, this little boy sees and hears his parents sticking up for themselves, fighting with clarity and respect, owning up to their faults without trying to weasel out of them, giving each other room to make mistakes without always being taken to task, taking risks, acting on their values rather than just talking about them, appreciating and loving each other and enjoying their relationship. When this little boy becomes a man he automatically conducts the majority of his life with integrity and honor.

For those of us who lacked good examples of accountability when we were growing up, cultivating integrity and honor begins with our fearless assessment of who we are and how we affect other human beings. Sometimes life invites us to do such an accounting and sometimes life grabs us by the throat and demands that we do it, as in the case of the man who went to prison for unintentionally killing another man in a drunken bar fight. He struggled and fought fiercely and bitterly for many years, angry at those who had imprisoned him, and even angrier beneath it all at those who hurt him when he was little. The angrier he became, the less anyone was willing to consider his parole, until one day he simply surrendered, at the age of forty-two. He entered the prison's alcohol rehabilitation program for the third time, but this time he did it voluntarily, not because his spirit was broken but because it finally demanded a voice—it had finally come to life after being dormant all those years.

Upon completing the program, he initiated a systematic process of becoming accountable to those he had hurt throughout his life. Without any court's suggestion or request, he began to make restitution or wrote contracts for restitution that he pledged to fulfill upon gaining his freedom and getting a job. The pledges were to himself alone. No one else knew about them. Upon his release from prison, he came to see us to help maintain his accountable behavior and to heal the old wounds that had accumulated from his painful childhood. He was a remarkable man, as close to a saint as we had ever personally encountered.

After two years of intermittent work with us, he came in for a session carrying several pieces of yellowed, creased old paper. He explained that these were the pledges of restitution he had written in prison, that he had shared them with no one, and that he had been living in near-poverty because he was putting money away and volunteering his services to make good on the pledges. He had brought them in to formally honor the people he had hurt, and to share his actions with us so that we could privately bear witness to what he had done, allowing his soul to rest at last. Our office was filled with warmth and light and tears, and a depth of dignity and honor that we have not felt since then. He knew that this had to be a private gesture because he had closed all of the other doors, leaving only this one to pass through.

Beyond Victim and Perpetrator

Power is an intriguing idea. Some of us desire it more than anything else. Others shrink from it. People say that power corrupts, but without any power, we would be hopeless victims. We prefer to look at it like anything else in the realm of human affairs—too little or too much, or the wrong kind, is the problem.

A woman we knew believed that if she ever admitted she was a victim of something she would dissolve into a puddle of shame. But if we are unable to *ever* admit our vulnerability, then we are doomed to be either victims or perpetrators, because part of being human is that we are vulnerable to those forces beyond our control. The most powerful woman in the world can still be a victim of cancer or a hurricane. A man believed that unless society legally acknowledged his victimhood by offering restitution of some sort, he would be trapped in it for all eternity, never to be happy or fulfilled, which is a formidable trap in itself. Some injustices are so horrible or so deliberate that they *require* restitution. But when you get fired because you express rage in the workplace, the fact that you may have been abused as a child does not require your employer to pay you for your perpetrations on your coworkers, even if you *feel* like a victim.

It may not be a surprise to hear this, but most people who are trapped in either the victim or the perpetrator roles are unaware of it. People have filters inside of them through which all experiences are interpreted. A therapist might say, "I think you have a lot of untapped resources and strengths," and the client might filter it into, "This therapist feels sorry for me and is really telling me that I'm not 'doing my life good enough.'" A woman's plane is delayed and the ticket agent cannot do anything because he isn't the pilot or mechanic, but the perpetrator cloaked in the victim's clothing sees this as a personal affront, saying to the agent, "You know damned well that you could do something to help me out here. If I were wealthy or famous you'd get that plane here on time for me!" A man declines an offer to join his associate for dinner because he has a previous commitment, and the associate who is responding from inside his perpetrator-hidden-as-victim role turns around in disgust, accusing the man of declining out of dislike for him. Confused by all of this pouting and posturing, the man may now be more guarded when approached by this associate in the future. This will reinforce the associate's distorted belief that this man doesn't like him.

Victim

With victimism comes a deeply felt sense of one's helplessness and powerlessness, which leads one to wait for what he wants or needs, to wait for others to change, to wait for life to get better. What looks like patience to some is actually a set of beliefs, feelings and behaviors that are screaming out from the depths, "There is something I deserve or need, but the only way I'll get it is if someone else reads my mind and then chooses to give it to me. I don't have the power to make it happen for myself." If you were to challenge such thinking you would encounter impenetrable resistance from the victim in the form of very rational arguments. A man might say, "I can't do anything about this horrible situation at work because my boss is an impossible jerk, and I've already put in for a transfer but there aren't any openings right now." Or a woman might say, "My partner keeps making nasty remarks to me in public, but there's nothing I can do because I've asked him to stop hundreds of times and it just doesn't do any good. He doesn't listen to me."

Even a political prisoner in an eight-by-eight cell has choices every day. He can run in place on Monday, start writing that novel he's always dreamed of on Tuesday, torment his captors on Wednesday, pray for them on Thursday, do sit-ups on Friday, eat on Saturday, fast on Sunday, meditate on Monday, cry on Tuesday, rage on Wednesday, share his life story with his fellow captives on Thursday, and on and on and on. People who maintain their choices in seemingly hopeless circumstances survive the best, but in our victimism, we surrender those choices for the safety of remaining unaccountable and emotionally "little." If you were to ask the victim if he would like things to be different, he would assert vociferously that it is all he dreams about. He might even get angry with you for implying that he wants to remain paralyzed in his life. But when you look at his behavior, beyond his vocal protests, all you can see is a person who is choosing to stay stuck for some reason.

To acknowledge our victimism—our paralysis based on

feelings and beliefs of powerlessness—is a formidable task. It is painful, embarrassing and scary to leave the miserable safety of victimism because for many it has become a way of life. But for many it can become a former way of life. One day a woman we know told us that she had decided to remove "If only . . ." and "But . . ." from her vocabulary when she spoke of difficulties in her life. With that simple realization, she was ready to acknowledge her victimhood and take her first shaky steps into adulthood.

Perpetrator

Jim Maddock and Noel Larson[54] were the first to note that the child (or children) in a painful family who grows up to be stuck primarily in the perpetrator role is the one who learned to protect himself by shutting off his feelings. This makes sense. If your father beats you, or your mother tries to flood you with all of her woes instead of sharing them with other adults, then one very *functional* way to survive is to shut it all down. But "shut it all down" quickly translates into: "I've been hurt enough. I'll never be hurt again. I'm not scared. Nothing scares me! I'm not hurt. Nothing hurts me! I'm not ashamed. I didn't do anything wrong—*you* did! I'm not lonely. I don't *need* anybody! I'm not sad. Life's hard, and that's all there is to it. People died in that tornado? Buck up!"

When we *dissociate*—disconnect from our feelings—too much, we become perpetrators for the simple reason that we shut off our ability to feel our softer feelings, which in turn cuts off our ability to empathize with others, resulting in statements like, "Aw, c'mon! I didn't mean anything by it.

I was just kidding! Don't take it so seriously!"

Whereas the primary belief in victimhood is that "no matter what I do, I'll never get what I want," the primary belief in the perpetrator role is that "as long as I stay 'strong' and stop worrying about 'them,' I can *get* what I want and never have to be vulnerable *or* accountable." In other words, as long as I stay angry, I'll be safe. *Anger equals safety.* So, I become "the tough one in the family." I'm the one who never makes a fuss when I break my arm. "Hey! Arms get broken! I don't sit back in a pool of fear when I have to give a speech. Hey! Go for it! I don't feel embarrassed if your feelings are hurt by my teasing. Hey! It was no big deal!"

What confuses some people is that *selective portions* of the victim or perpetrator roles are very healthy. It is healthy to surrender in the face of the uncontrollable, just as it is healthy in many situations to "buck up" and "go for it" when your anxiety is nudging you in the direction of giving up. In other words, remember the extremes. The problem with *always being tough* is that it closes the door to an entire universe of experiences. As we explained earlier, the deepest levels of intimacy occur at the level of our weakness, but only if we are inherently strong and integrated. Being strong *all the time* precludes sharing those ineffable moments when we find ourselves shedding tears at the beginning of the second movement of Beethoven's *Fifth Symphony,* or when our partner realizes how hard it was for her to feel important when she was growing up.

Always being tough means that my lover will never see me cry at a funeral. He will never see me admit that I am ashamed and saddened because I yelled at the cab driver on the way to the airport. He won't feel the depth of my soul as I grapple with the impending departure of our youngest child as she graduates and goes off into the world. No matter how good of a person I am—and I probably am a good person, because most people are—my lover and my friends won't get to connect with me at the level both they and I would like. Ironically, because I am so competent and caring-at-a-distance, the people closest to me will be mired in conflict about their relationship with me. They will want more intimacy with me, but they won't want me to go to the other extreme and become weak and ineffectual.

Maddock and Larson[55] also observed that people who are caught in the perpetrator role are actually more fragile— more brittle—than people who are caught in the victim role, which on the surface seems counterintuitive. But stop for a moment and reflect on this statement. What is all that thrashing and lashing and defensiveness about, if not the stark terror of abandonment and loss? People don't rage and pound on their loved ones because they are strong. And they certainly don't do it in most cases because they are "evil." When a man beats up his spouse after she says she's going back to college, it's usually because he's terrified that he'll lose her—either because his thoughts run wild and he imagines her falling for some other guy in one of her classes, or in a more generic sense, because he fears that if he loses his absolute power over her, she'll leave. Perpetration is about fear, and the only way out of this distorted power-bind is to (1) grow up, and (2) start using the word "and."

If you turn to the table of contents for a moment and look at the heading for part III, you will see that it reads: *"And"*

Is a Powerful Word. Whenever you are lost in the "emotional woods," stop yourself and remember that in most cases, the path to home is about six or seven degrees away. You can fight and squirm and defend yourself until the cows come home. You can spit and punch and rail at life itself. Struggle and strength are good. You're okay. If toughness and "guts" and the ability to tolerate huge amounts of discomfort are your strengths, by all means, keep those strengths, as long as you can add the "and." Once you are able to do that, you will be able to say:

> *I am strong,* and *I can cry at this funeral, because I need to grieve. I fear my wife's return to college,* and *I can talk to her about it without "being weak" or "giving her all my power so she doesn't respect me." I can do these things and maintain my "self" and my identity—who I am—and it will set me free. I can be free of my demons, because when I let my anger rest for a moment, that entire other universe that I have been shoving down and away can breathe and come alive, and then I can, too.*

On Value: "I Guess We See It Differently"

Feeling like you have value is one of the most important parts of a really great relationship. Feeling like your ideas or feelings are unimportant is one of the most destructive things that can happen. But how do really great partners handle those situations where they disagree? One of the most useful and powerful responses that you can have at your disposal is to say, "I guess we see it differently." It not only addresses the question of owning your own part, but it also removes disputes from the realm of win or lose.

"Needing to be right" is such a primitive yet destructive expression in a relationship. As we've shown throughout this book, if you always defer to the other person, you end up disappearing, and if you never defer, you end up being a bully. A couple we worked with came in for their appointment right in the middle of a fight about whether it would be better for them to both go to the same business seminar, or for one to go to a different one and thereby gather more information for their company. At one level, they were having differences of opinion about how to spend company money, how to best nurture their relationship and about efficiency. At another level, it had quickly gone to a core level of whether his way was better than hers, and even deeper, whether he had more value than she because he was right and she was wrong.

Finally, the wife took charge of the disagreement by saying in a very calm, determined, and not the least bit angry, condescending or whiny tone, "I guess we just see it differently."

Her husband stopped in "mid-rant," looked at her with a surprised and almost mirthful expression, and asked, "What does *that* mean?" He smiled. Before she could answer, he added, "Okay. Okay. You're right. There *is* no right answer here. You're right."

In a display of mock amazement, she laughed and declared, "Oh my God! My husband just said I'm *right* about something! Mark the calendar! It's a miracle!"

He smiled and laughed.

We said, "So, you can *both* have value, even if you disagree completely about something."

He smiled again. "Yes, it feels much better. It's much *easier* to do it that way."

Obviously, you can't use this strategy all the time. Sometimes people have to argue about something until it's "all argued out," and they can come to some sort of compromise. Sometimes one of them *is* right and is correct in not giving in. Either way, it is important not to lose sight of the fact that if both people do not feel valued—if they don't both feel like what they think and feel matters to the other—then the relationship is in trouble.

In *Take Back Your Marriage*,[56] psychologist Bill Doherty, author of *The Intentional Family* and *Take Back Your Kids*, describes a number of invaluable ways that people can restore the shine to a faded relationship even if it appears there is little hope. He discusses many of the ways that marriages get into trouble in the first place, including putting your children first and your marriage last—which was one of our "7 Worst Things (Good) Parents Do." Bill uses one term throughout much of his work. The word is "intentional." We like this word because it describes what we choose—i.e., what we *will* ourselves to do. If you consciously intend to do something, it will be likely to happen. If you are consciously mindful of things, you will most likely notice them. It implies that we have the power of choice and free will. It implies that we are responsible for our actions and our lives. It says what August Wilson says in *Two Trains Running*: We *are* accountable.[57]

16

Let Disappointment Enrich You

"... We don't believe that you should offer it for
publication. It is diffuse and nonintegral with
neither very much plot development
nor character development."

—Rejection letter to William Faulkner

Please the Teacher and Win the Prize?

Psychologist Stephen Gilligan recalled a wonderful personal story from when he was a nineteen-year-old psychology student attending a small five-day workshop at the Arizona home of world-famous psychiatrist and hypnotherapist Milton Erickson. Wanting so badly to be liked by Erickson and to be invited back to study with him,

257

the young Gilligan stayed up each night, working on a fable that he then courageously read in front of everyone. Erickson used a lot of metaphor and storytelling in his work, and Gilligan waited anxiously for a positive reaction from this man he idolized. As he finished his fable, the reaction was . . .

. . . Silence. Erickson looked at me for a long time, said nothing, then looked away and almost casually started talking about something else. For the rest of the meeting, he ignored me. I was utterly devastated.[58]

As everyone was leaving, and "in a quavering voice," Gilligan asked, "What is your answer?"

Erickson came back with, "What is the question?"

"May I come back and study with you?"

Gilligan wrote that Erickson's face warmed, and he beamed as he said, "Of course. Why didn't you just ask?"

The brilliance of this tale sends chills down our spines because it captures so many things in such a small space. Gilligan used it in his article to help show that for a therapist to be truly effective, she needs to be able to "reach out to the client from her own deepest core." He pointed out how Erickson had "demolished his pretensions" by reacting the way he did to Gilligan's attempts to please.

We like the story for many reasons. One reason we like it is that it demonstrates the immeasurable value of disappointment in our lives. It is only through disappointment that we are able to grow. Had Erickson said, "I like your fable. It is a lot like the ones I use in therapy. You have learned well, Grasshopper," what would Gilligan have learned?

The Analyst

Narcissism is a natural part of being human. What we do with it determines the depth and peace of our lives. In one of the most touching stories we have ever read, Adam Gopnik, writing in *The New Yorker*, shared elements of his lengthy psychoanalysis, which he introduced as:

> *. . . one of the last times a German-born analyst, with a direct laying on of hands from Freud, spent forty-five minutes twice a week for six years discussing, in a small room on Park Avenue decorated with Motherwell posters, the problems of a "creative" New York neurotic.* [59]

Gopnik proceeded to describe, in elegant, understated terms, one of the most subtle and finest relationships that we have ever been privileged to witness. With an uncanny ability to portray the paradoxes and ironies involved by writing with the same structure and style as that of this unfolding relationship, he ended his engaging story with a description of his own angry disappointment with the much awaited "final wisdom" of his longtime mentor, which turned out to be profoundly simple: "In retrospect, life has many worthwhile aspects."

After his analyst's death, Gopnik tenderly noted that:

> *He is inside me. In moments of crisis or panic, I sometimes think that I have his woolen suit draped around my shoulders, even in August. Sometimes in ordinary moments I almost think that I have become him.* [60]

The Power of Embracing Disappointment

The power that permeates the stories above resides in the universal experience of being a vulnerable human being who desperately wants to be connected to those whom we value "because we need them." We don't care if the nerdy kid in school likes us. We want the cool kid to like us. We don't need every adult to like us. We want our *dad* to like us. We are essentially very powerful, very "big" creatures, who have a very "little" part inside of us who wants an even bigger creature to lay on those hands. For this reason, we especially like Friedrich Schleiermacher's definition of God as *the ultimate being upon whom we can depend.* If we can actually trust that someone more powerful than us—Dad, Mom, our therapist—*values* us, then we can start to trust ourselves and not need so much.

But being human, this "need to need" will never go away completely, and therefore we will always struggle with disappointment. Either I am all-powerful, and therefore I will never need again, or I am not, and then no matter how powerful I become, I will always need something. This is the ultimate bind that is captured in our narcissism.

Another bind is that in wanting to be special like the people whom we idealize, we initially fail to see that true greatness is always carefully wrapped in genuine humility, as represented so elegantly by Austrian psychoanalyst Wilhelm Stekel:

> *The mark of the immature man is that he wants to die nobly for a cause. The mark of the mature man is that he wants to live humbly for one.*[61]

The power of embracing disappointment is seen in the little girl who loses the swimming competition and finds that her parents are supportive, without fawning. Life goes on. The expected ecstasy isn't there. Not from winning. But not from being a loser, either! *Life just . . . life just . . . just . . . goes* on? *I was* so *hoping to be special, and if I can't win and be special, I at least want to* lose *and be special! But they aren't fawning over me! They must not love me. Ah! There we have it! I can be special if they don't love me! I can wallow in my misery. My parents don't love me! Listen to me, world! My parents don't love me!*

Of course, her parents *do* love her, and thus her struggle becomes one of either accepting that she can't have everything she wants, or becoming bitter, angry and disappointed that life is "so unfair." Life *is* unfair sometimes. In fact, there is enough unfairness in the world to keep us busy focusing on it for a lifetime, if we so choose. But what sort of choice would *that* be? I would certainly be an unhappy person. But maybe there's an advantage to that—a payoff. I could be the tortured poet, filled with misery and angst, filling my notebooks with expressions of my cynical, dark interpretation of the world. Or I could simply elicit more than my fair share of pity from those around me—*that* could be a decent payoff, especially if I am secretly starved for connection with others.

But what if I, this little girl, eventually come to accept that my parents *do* love me, that I am okay even if I didn't win the swimming competition, and that if I listen to the hum of the universe all around me, I may actually learn something that can only be learned in this way. Now, *that* would be something!

Disappointment is what happens when we grow up and

discover that our father and mother are flawed. Enrichment comes when we can open our hearts and minds and souls and love them anyway. It comes when we thought we were going to "die nobly for some great cause" but wound up, as Stekel said, "living humbly for one." It is contained in the universe of difference between being dependent on others' evaluations of us, and graciously appreciating it when others pay us a legitimate compliment. This paradoxical enrichment is the ability to appreciate Shakespeare's elegant words:

> *My plenteous joys*
> *Wanton in fullness, seek to hide themselves*
> *In drops of sorrow*[62]

The rejection slip quoted at the beginning of this chapter is a common part of a writer's existence. William Faulkner received close to a dozen rejections for what has become his most famous novel, *The Sound and the Fury*. Robert Pirsig's *Zen and the Art of Motorcycle Maintenance* received 121 rejections before being published and then going on to sell over 3 million copies. John Steinbeck, one of the greatest writers in modern literature, described how he faced the adversity and potential disappointment of writing:

> *When I face the desolate impossibility of writing five hundred pages a sick sense of failure falls on me and I know I can never do it. This happens every time. Then gradually I write one page and then another. One day's work is all I can permit myself to contemplate and I eliminate the possibility of ever finishing.*

Margaret Mitchell's *Gone with the Wind* was rejected by two dozen publishers with statements like, "The public is not interested in Civil War stories."[63]

Richness vs. Shallowness

One of the most enriching experiences in life is to want something more than anything in the world, to have it within your reach, and then to have it slip between your fingers at the last moment. When we tell couples that they need to "cultivate their disappointments," we don't mean that they should intentionally sabotage each other's happiness. That would be mean-spirited to say the least. What we mean is that life at its deepest is filled with mystery and wonder. It is both light and dark. Embracing the richness and depth of human experience includes grappling with the dark recesses within ourselves, as well as the seeming darkness in life.

One of the paradoxes of being human is that the more we pretend that life doesn't have a harsher side—the more Pollyannaish we are—the more likely we will cause great unhappiness in ourselves and others. In addition to being nominated for a Pulitzer Prize, poet, actor and playwright Maya Angelou has the distinction of being one of America's most banned writers. She has written about the fact that she was raped at the age of eight, and her candor about such topics has frightened some people. In a recent interview she said:

Quite often parents tell their children, "I've never done anything wrong." They pretend that not only are there not any skeletons in the closet, they don't even have closets. When I found out I was one of the most banned writers in the United States, I felt sorry for the children and sorry for parents because they couldn't have read ten pages of the book of mine and not understood. I wrote about rape, and it's happening all

*over and with more frequency now. Not reading about it
doesn't make it go away.*[64]

When we let our inner complexity blossom, it gives us a
set of lenses that lets life be three-dimensional. Human
beings are seen as basically good and also flawed, rather than
all good or all bad. Tragedy is accepted as that part of life
over which we do not have control, and yet our innate drive
to know and understand creation helps us master more and
more of the world around us. We have large brains for that
very purpose. Those same large brains have come to accept
the rather humorous fact that the more we discover, the
more we discover that we don't know. The hackneyed saying that "life's a bitch and then you die" might be spoken
for any number of reasons, but for people who are not yet
complex enough inside, it is spoken because it is truly
believed. This is unfortunate and entirely unnecessary.

The way to reconcile the many paradoxes and ironies in
the world is to yield to the fact that life is bigger than we
are, which is what constitutes the "deepening power" of disappointment. The ultimate disappointment for human
beings is that we all die someday, which is the finale to a
series of "little deaths" all along life's way. When a friend
moves away or you lose your job or you don't get the part in
the play that you were just sure you'd won hands down,
there is an emptiness and an ache that lingers. It is the feel
and the sound of our imaginations bumping into a reality
that had something else in mind.

When it comes to couples, the reality that we bump into
is often our partner. A woman may want a man to take an

interest in her horses, and he says he will, but it never materializes. Secretly he's saying to himself, *She wants me involved with her horses. She takes no interest in my desire to go camping in the wilderness. Why should I?*

After awhile, she starts to nag him about it. Then she lectures him. Then she nags him some more. "I really want you to take an interest in my riding. It's very important to me."

He snaps back, "And wilderness camping is important to me."

Then she snaps back, "You know I can't go wilderness camping. I'm terrified of snakes, I am horribly allergic to poison oak, and I freeze to death if it goes below fifty degrees. I'd love to, really, but I just can't."

Then he thinks to himself, *That may be true. Okay. But I just don't feel like this relationship is balanced. It feels like she gets everything she wants. I've been waiting for her to go wilderness camping with me ever since we got married four years ago.*

When people dig their heels in like this, it is because they actually believe that if they don't get what they want from their partner, the relationship will then be worth less than before. In some cases that might be true, but in many cases, just the opposite is true. If the man in this story were to acknowledge the physical dangers associated with wilderness camping for his partner and then just surrender to the fact that she will never be able to go with him, then a whole world of choices opens up to him. He can leave her and find a new partner who likes to go camping. He can stay and never once show any interest in her riding whatsoever. He could stay, learn to enjoy wilderness camping without her, and not participate in her riding, but not in a punitive

way—there is, you know, an obvious difference between
the punitive and nonpunitive reactions here. He could also
stay and take up riding, and in the process, open up the
relationship to some heretofore astonishing connections in
their relationship. We always have choices.

Life is filled with bounteous joys, depending on how you
perceive your world. Some people believe that they should
have what they want when they want it. Some people
believe that they will never get anything they want. Most of
us have something that we want so badly that we can almost
taste it. The 50 percent of the nation who wanted so desperately for Al Gore to win the 2000 election sat by and
watched, stunned, as he ended his concession speech so
gracefully that it could have gotten him elected had he
acted like that during the presidential debates:

*As for the battle that ends tonight, I do believe, as my father
once said, that no matter how hard the loss, defeat may serve
as well as victory to shake the soul and let the glory out.*

Life, Death and Disappointment

Our literature, oral histories and religions are filled with
the value of disappointment in tempering and deepening
us. The Bible, Talmud, Koran, Greek and Roman my-
thology, Native American spiritual wisdom, Freudian psychology, and authors from Shakespeare to Robert Bly and
Thomas Moore all embrace the importance of trials and
tribulations, rituals of initiation and awakening, in our
quest for meaning and maturity.

A man says, "I deserve to have the things I want in life. I deserve to be treated well by others. I deserve to be praised for my work. I deserve to be loved. I deserve to have someone pay when things don't work out." It is certainly true that we deserve some things in life, but when we have a distorted sense of entitlement we get terribly confused, believing that some force in life is out to hurt us when we don't get all that we want when we want it. The inability to find the perspective between reality and our desires can result in deeply felt misery and the experience of continual betrayal. An adult with this distortion may become demanding, self-absorbed and manipulative because he believes that he should be happy all the time, which is impossible for anyone.

As an adult struggles with issues of distorted entitlement, she is invited into the clarifying challenge of coming to terms with her disappointment, which when embraced, permits her to turn a frustrating, scary, miserable life into a full, satisfying, peaceful one. No matter how smart we are, or how wealthy, clever or powerful, life will always offer us the chance to become full through our disappointments. They are some of the primary threads that are woven into our lives, and without them, our lives would lack brilliance and definition.

Look into the eyes of a very old woman who has struggled with life, relished in its ecstasy, and come to terms with all of its depth, harshness, forgiveness and yielding. Her face may be creased with twists and turns that tell a multitude of stories about childhood insecurities, painful first loves, children born and friends dying, a lover beyond all imagination, missed opportunities, risks well-chosen, losses embraced with grace and dignity, tolerance and wisdom purely earned. Her eyes, while fading, are bright in all that they have seen and taken in, and her soul is full and ready for the next challenge, which gives her peace. She is a living testament to the value inherent in facing disappointment with patience and courage. Even in our fast-moving high-technology world, we still find the precious core of awe inside of us when we come face-to-face with an aged soul who has lived well. Few experiences reveal as much power to us.

When someone is touched by grace as he nears life's end so that he can finally acknowledge his disappointment after so many years of pretending that none existed, it is especially poignant. An old man we knew had lived a hard, lonely life forged during the Great Depression and strengthened in its isolation by a difficult marriage and alienation from his children, whom he had hurt deeply when they were growing up. He had never honored the darkness in his soul that had kept him from celebrating his children's birthdays and life transitions, which resulted in an unspoken chasm between him and those he fathered and raised. And then one day, a few years before he died, this man watched as his grandson's home filled with friends who came to surprise him in honor of his birthday. Even with thirty teenagers noisily celebrating in his daughter's house, his tears were easily noticed and welcomed as warmly as his grandson's guests. He didn't stay at the party very long because he wearied easily, but that mattered little. The gift that he needed to give and receive had been manifested and accepted. It was enough.

Aside from the personal fear of one's death that emerges from somewhere deep inside most of us in middle age, nothing is as painful as the disappointments that we face along the way. A man's first marriage ends with such pain and grief that he wonders if he will ever stop hurting. A woman loses her first child in a miscarriage and feels as if her very soul has been torn from inside of her. The career that you thought would be the perfect one from time immemorial turns out to have limitations. The thought of starting over is demoralizing at first, and yet it is the acceptance and embracing of these ordinary losses that eventually heals our fear of death, allowing us to finally live our lives with a peace that we never thought possible.

A man who is still a child will be plagued by unending inner turmoil each time he discovers that he is surrounded by imperfect human beings and an imperfect world. He will either revile or idolize each person he meets, and those whom he idolizes will eventually fall prey to his painful need for perfection. Over and over, he will find someone to idealize, and then almost as quickly, his unconscious mind will begin searching for flaws until this latest hero has fallen from grace, leaving another void of disappointment in the soul of the beholder. A grown-up will see the limitations, feel the disappointment, accept his hero's flaws, release his need for perfection and then acknowledge his hero's gifts. This lets the hero become a human being with value and dignity while allowing the beholder to be realistic and appreciative, and in the process, the beholder comes a little closer to finding peace with the thought of his own death.

So it seems that it is not always in our best interests to achieve the happiness that we are seeking in the moment. Some people struggle and fight so fiercely at one level of existence that they prevent themselves from moving to the next level of existence where the waters are so much smoother and clearer. Coming to terms with our disappointments isn't always a matter of keeping a stiff upper lip and pushing our pain deep inside so that we can maintain an aura of grace while we secretly bleed. It is actually quite ordinary to appreciate what we do not have for the simple reason that by doing so we can be invited down into a deeper level of existence, beyond the surface struggles in which we had become so embroiled. When we are able to do this, life suddenly seems simpler, brighter, deeper, richer and more complex all at the same time.

In the story of *The Man, the Woman and the Sea*, their struggle with the frustrations and disappointments about each other was rewarded with a brilliant flash of mutual vulnerability that deepened their love for one another in a way that surprised both of them. For a long time, the man believed that his relationship with the woman would be doomed unless she eventually relented and took up ocean swimming with him, only to find that their relationship became a lifetime of love because she didn't. The result of their struggle was unpredictable, unplanned and uncontrolled, demonstrating that life is full of wondrous twists and turns that can deepen us and bring us joy in ways we never imagined, but only if we are willing to risk and reach out for what we want at the time, struggle hard and then let go to leave room for something even better.

As we find true peace in all of these disappointments along the way, the inevitability of our own death loses its terror, which allows us to embrace and fully enjoy life.

Part V

Do You Have a Story?

*Five short stories, written over
a period of two or three years,
caused me to invest nine
dollars and fifty cents in
dimes to rent a pay typewriter
in a basement library typing
room and finish the short
novel in just nine days.*

Ray Bradbury
1993, Introduction to the fortieth-anniversary
edition of *Fahrenheit 451*

17

Keola Beamer

He lei keakea noho maila I ka mauna
Ka mauna ki'eki'e I luna ku kilakila
Kilakila 'o luna 'o I ke ao.

—Nona Beamer[65]

A man we know enjoys listening to the music of Keola Beamer, the Hawaiian slack key guitar master. In the liner notes of one of these CDs, the artist wrote:

I keep a journal of the things that happen in my life. As the years went by, I discovered that words placed limitations on the depth of my experiences. I came to believe that words were rather crude instruments. Music has since become my way of communicating these feelings.[66]

Our friend has a history that explains why he happens to be drawn to this music, although he had forgotten it for a long time. His mother was born in 1914 and grew up on a tiny, struggling ranch out west. Her father was a good man, alcoholic, and like so many, a friend to all except his wife. Her mother worked herself into the ground keeping hearth and home in place while her father took a job in town where he could be a shining star. Our friend's mother wept as she shared with him how, as a little girl, she would sit with her own mother and listen to her mother's dreams of going to Hawaii.

When Webley Edwards began broadcasting his live radio program, "Hawaii Calls," from the Moana Hotel in 1935, mother and daughter let themselves be transported from the sadness and burden of the mother's daily life to the sounds of the gentle surf washing up on Waikiki Beach. It was the 1930s. Her mother didn't have the advantage of today's psychology. She didn't know how damaging it can be for a parent to rest her weary head on a child's shoulder—even a grown child. And so our friend's mother carried her own mother's longing for a better life and love in the form of a longing for Hawaii, a place her mother never got to see because she died from overwork at a relatively early age.

When our friend was a child, his mother told him of her love for Hawaii and for her longing to go there. She listened to "Hawaii Calls" every week. When she finally made it there at the age of forty-four, she wept and wept on the long flight across the Pacific. Our friend was confused by his feelings, and at the same time, was gathered up by the family's subsequent intoxication with the Islands. Themes nestle into our lives unobtrusively and then just live there from generation to generation. He traveled there with his family many times, and then he went off into his own life. He had other dreams to pursue and puzzles to unravel.

When he was a little boy, he had been smothered by his grandmother's sadness, and by her longings for a healthy love. But he never knew his grandmother. She died before he was born. His grandmother's sadness was carried by his mother. He didn't even realize that his grandmother was a part of it. He was in a trance. Tradewinds. The bright clean smell of a fresh banana that he hadn't smelled since he was a young boy. Humidity that wasn't oppressive. And then there was that damned Hawaiian music. He went on with his life, assured that he was finished with that particular chapter.

He married, had children, even visited Hawaii, but it was clear this time—it was with the love of his life, and they were grown up. No confusing feelings. They found a place there that they could both feel passionate about despite their differences. It was magic for them both. They didn't go back for a long time. Raising kids, careers, other places to see. It's a big world. Their children grew up. They started to think of retirement, although it was still a long way off.

And then their grown daughter sent them a Keola Beamer CD. It wasn't a big deal. She thought they might enjoy it. He and the woman he adored listened to the music. It was soothing. Pleasant. They had hectic, fulfilling lives. As they made the leisurely drive to their vacation home one summer afternoon, a poignant wave of sadness and joy and relief and tropical mystery brushed by his consciousness. He looked over at his wife and felt the warmth of their relationship being bathed in haunting Polynesian melodies, smiled and thought that there must be a story at least as interesting, if not more so, that sustained Keola Beamer in the same way.

Whether you write it or sing it or paint it or sculpt it, we encourage you to find your story and share it with the people you love.

18

Ray Bradbury

We have been made accountable for this gift
of life so that we will see and know and believe
and celebrate! We are witnesses! We must witness
and celebrate, every day of our lives!
How can you miss this wonderful show?!
We give it purpose by living and creating!

—Ray Bradbury, 1999
Address to the Hennepin County Library Foundation

In celebration of Rich's (JCF's brother) fiftieth birthday, we were strolling past the shops in Laguna Beach with him and our sister and her husband and noticed a line of people in front of the little bookshop there. Curious, we ascended the short flight of stairs to the plaza above, where there in the warm Southern California sun sat Ray Bradbury, autographing fortieth-anniversary copies of his masterful indictment of censorship, *Fahrenheit 451*. We bought Rich a copy for his birthday and one for ourselves as we chatted briefly with this distinguished, warm, enthusiastic, white-haired, energetically "young" man.

Six years later, as we listened to Minnesota Public Radio on the way to work, tears welled up in our eyes as we heard a remarkable address to the Library Foundation of Hennepin County by Ray Bradbury, in which he discussed in the most touching, engaging, delightful, moving terms many of the key influences that eventually determined the direction and scope of his prolific career. The man who wrote *The Martian Chronicles, Something Wicked This Way Comes, Dandelion Wine, The Illustrated Man* and *Fahrenheit 451* had also been invited to spend a year in Ireland with John Huston and company to write the screenplay for *Moby Dick*! At the time of his address, he had published over five hundred short stories, novels, plays and poems, beginning with his first at the age of twenty.

It wasn't just his warmth or good-natured humor or the sheer expanse and depth of his accomplishments over the decades that captured our souls for a moment in time. It was our appreciation of the depth and awe-inspiring power beneath the early experiences and recollections that shape people's lives. For him, the first was when his grammar school classmates made fun of him for collecting Buck Rogers comic books. He said he "belonged in the future," but succumbed to the taunts and destroyed his collection. After going into a period of depression and despair, he realized that he had only one option open to him—to start collecting Buck Rogers comic books and start living in the future again!

The second was when he was a boy of twelve in Waukeegan, Illinois. The carnival was in town at the same time that one of his favorite uncles had died. One of the carnival acts, Mr. Electrico, had befriended Bradbury after touching the tip of his nose with his electrostatically charged sword and commanding, "Live forever!" On the way to the wake, after the funeral, he urgently demanded that his father stop the car, and he jumped out, avoiding the wake, seeking out Mr. Electrico instead. They sat by the lake that night and talked "great philosophies of life," and he was transformed. He stood by the calliope and wept as "Beautiful Ohio" played hauntingly, and "I knew that something important had happened in my life. Within three weeks, I started writing short stories—every day of my life, for sixty-five years. . . ."

After that, he corresponded with Mr. Electrico, who turned out to be a defrocked minister from Cairo, Illinois. Years later, as the film version of *Something Wicked This Way Comes* was about to be released, the Disney people asked if he would like to find Mr. Electrico, and Bradbury said he would love to. He said it was one of his bigger disappointments that they were unable to locate the man who was responsible for literally electrifying his writing career.

Celebration of the electricity that surges throughout life is what Bradbury's career has been about. Over fifteen years ago, the Smithsonian Institution invited Bradbury to provide consultation for their planetarium show, which he said was "putting people to sleep." He told them that a planetarium should be like a synagogue or a church where people are inspired rather than simply educated. He said that if people were inspired about the mysteries of the universe, they would go out and buy the books and study. He wrote a twenty-eight-page script for their show entitled "The Great Shout of the Universe," which he said was returned to him with twenty-eight pages of criticisms and corrections. He eventually convinced them to buy him out of his contract, and he moved the show to the Los Angeles Planetarium, where, narrated by James Whitmore, it has run successfully every day for fifteen years. He described the "Great Shout" as "the mysteries at the center of everything that we can't solve, but we can witness and celebrate."

Where you come from—the things that drive you—is part of the "great shout" inside each one of us. To share pieces of your story with your partner, and to be curious and to listen to your partner with intention and discernment, is what electrifies relationships until the day that "death do us part."

APPENDIX A

The Early "Cup-Fillers" in Detail[67]

Erik Erikson's brilliant work has spawned decades of research into all aspects of human development, but none more so than on the development of identity. His work has also generated much research to support his assertion that until we have a good sense of who we are, our capacity for mature, enduring intimacy will be very limited.

By *identity* we mean self-definition. We mean self-knowledge and a commitment to a set of values, beliefs, behaviors and a lifestyle. Our identities include what we like and don't like, what risks we are willing to take, what we believe in, both religiously and philosophically, as well as politically and scientifically. Identity includes our sexual behaviors and feelings, our career choices, our satisfaction or dissatisfaction with them, and whether we choose to be parents or not. Whether we choose to go to church or not. Whether we choose to be in a spouse or lover-type relationship. What we like to do with our free time. Whether we are alcoholic or cocaine-addicted or sexually addicted or running addicts is also part of our identities, as is whether or not we are recovering from these addictions or are still acting them out.

Even in a very healthy family, the task of growing up and leaving home with a clear identity of our own is a challenge. Somewhere between the ages of eighteen and thirty-two or so, our main developmental task is to come to terms with who we are as autonomous adults. This task hinges on the relatively successful fulfillment of four earlier developmental challenges, and incorporates the issues and skills from those earlier stages. The four stages leading up to the *identity crisis* are:

birth–18 months	Trust vs. Mistrust
18 months–3 years	Autonomy vs. Shame and Doubt
3 years–6 years	Initiative vs. Guilt
6 years–18+ years	Industry vs. Inferiority

These stages represent what Erikson called *psychosocial crises,* but they can also be called *accomplishments.* Each one builds upon all of the earlier ones. This means that if the stones at the base of the foundation are weak, or nearly nonexistent, the entire structure will be weak. If we have developmental stages that were handled less than ideally early in life, then we will run into a lot of trouble later as we try to grow up and become adults.

These crises or stages are broadly defined. They are labeled according to when they *first* became a major task in our lives. As you peruse the list of stages, you will see that they are tasks and challenges that face all of us throughout our lives, not just when they first appear. And remember that each stage and the skills that we learn as we pass through it become incorporated into the later stages. For example, the Initiative vs. Guilt stage includes issues of Trust and Autonomy. These Trust and Autonomy issues are age-appropriate, though, so it does not mean that to take the initiative we have to go back to infancy and breast-feed again, or that we have to learn how to walk again.

Trust vs. Mistrust: Birth to Eighteen Months

The first challenge facing us as human beings is to develop a basic sense of trust in the world. This means that we are left with a feeling that we can rely on those we need, that the world is basically a safe place to be and that we can survive. If our basic needs for food, shelter, affection and touch are met during early infancy, then we most likely will develop a sense of trust that things will work out in the end, even if we don't get what we need right away.

To develop trust, a little child does not have to be the tyrant of the house, demanding and getting everything he wants on the spot. If he is told that he will have to wait a few minutes until dinner is ready, or that he cannot have everything that he sees in a store, it will not erode his basic sense of trust. In fact, if we go overboard in giving things to our children, we actually undermine their sense of trust because we are setting them up to live in a world that doesn't exist. Nobody in this world gets everything he wants when he wants it. One of the most important themes of development throughout our entire lives begins right here, in the first stage: *Too much or too little of what we need is not good.*

Things that leave a child with a basic sense of *mistrust* about the world and themselves include overt physical or emotional abuse, neglect or abandonment. These are extremes. The more subtle forces that operate during this stage are inconsistent care (babysitting or daycare do not have to be inconsistent), tension and stress in parents that are communicated by the inability to be nurturing, spontaneous or comfortable with our infants. Too much overt conflict can upset young children, and overprotective parents who do not allow their young children to explore their world and their own bodies in normal ways can get in the way.

Infants need to learn that they can depend on us and that the world will not always give them what they want, and that they can still be "okay" about it. They do not need to be scared, spoiled, neglected or abused. A basic sense of mistrust leaves us with abandonment issues.

Autonomy vs. Shame and Doubt: Eighteen Months to Three Years

The issue to be resolved here is one of separateness, individuation or differentiation. Between eighteen months and three years of age, our children become mobile, and they learn the power of language for defining their separateness (the word "no!" for example). Their task is to begin to become autonomous while still feeling safe and trusting the world.

Our two-year-olds toddle off to explore things by themselves. They exert their will. They get into power struggles with us. And because they are still so vulnerable and dependent upon us, they need to be able to do this and still know that they can run back to us for comfort if their independence leads them into things that are scary or hurtful.

Imagine yourself at two, running into the house in tears, crying that "a big dog walked through the yard and growled at me!" The dog represents a threat to our sense of autonomy: "I can't go out into the world by myself because it's too dangerous." If your dad or mom simply affirms you and your feelings by saying, "Boy, I'll bet that was scary," and makes you feel safe again by giving you a hug and letting you have your feelings without being judgmental, then soon you will be ready to go back into the world again.

If, on the other hand, your parents *shame* you ("Big boys don't cry," "I told you not to go outside by yourself"), or simply aren't available enough to you during these times (either physically or emotionally), then you will begin to internalize shame and doubt.

Likewise, you can experience shame and doubt if you are too restricted in your attempts to be a separate individual. Parents who mean well but who are overprotective of you never give you the chance to separate from them. If your parents are too permissive, giving you few guidelines on how to behave in the world outside of your home, you can wind up feeling shame and doubt. Parents who let their children climb on the furniture, frequently break things and generally tyrannize the household produce children who often get shamed when they go to other people's homes or when they go to school.

Again, the rule of thumb here is one of balance. We need to set limits and boundaries for our children at this age, but we also need to allow enough freedom and safety for them to want to begin separating from us.

Initiative vs. Guilt: Three to Six Years

This stage has a lot to do with our ability to start things, make things happen and stretch beyond our current capabilities. Those of us who are "stuck," who can't get out of a rut, who can't make decisions, have issues with this stage.

Between three and six years of age, we want to become more like adults. We want to go into the kitchen and cook something the way Mom and Dad do. Or we want to go into the garage and get the saw and build something. We want to initiate things. This has much to do with self-expansion, of going beyond. If you think about it, anytime we try to initiate something on our own, there is always the possibility of someone else feeling put out, let down, disappointed or "hurt." When they let us know about it, we feel guilty.

Dad gets a bee in his bonnet and decides to tear out the wall in the kitchen and do some remodeling while Mom is on a business trip. Mom comes home, doesn't like it and says, "How could you begin such a major change in my kitchen without first consulting me?" Dad feels some shame, but he will also feel guilt. He has "done something wrong." He feels like he has violated a moral principle of some kind.

The task at ages three to six is to begin internalizing principles of right and wrong, but not to the detriment of our ability to initiate things. If my children try to rebuild the engine of my car at this age, I need to convey to them that this is inappropriate behavior because they aren't old enough to do it properly, and besides, it's "my" car, not "theirs." It's how I convey that message that is so important.

If I say, "You really let down Dad. I am surprised that you would do this. You really hurt me by doing it," my children will indeed not do it again. But if I use this method of discipline on a regular basis, I will produce very well-behaved children who won't be able to get themselves out of a wet paper bag when they are adults. They will be "nice," but that's about it. They will be filled with guilt and indecision. They will always focus on who will be affected by their actions without ever considering their own needs or feelings. They will become overfocused on not violating all of these rules they internalize—big rules, middle-sized rules and pointless tiny rules.

Industry vs. Inferiority:
Six to Eighteen+ Years

This stage involves developing a sense of competence and confidence around those skills necessary for survival in your culture. These skills include the Three Rs, but go well beyond them. Certainly, we need academic skills to get by in this world, but all too often the range of skills that are reinforced in our schools and at home is painfully narrow. Not every child will be a whiz at math, English or physics. Not every child will become another Picasso or Beethoven. Some children will become excellent mechanics, if allowed to be. Others will become well-adjusted accountants. Others, plumbers. These school-age years are critical for a child's sense of worth. They are also critical for a child's ability to identify with, and bond with, older people who know how to do things. So it is a compliment to us, and to our child, if he forms an attachment to a friend's dad who is showing him how to build things. It is okay if our daughter likes her English teacher and gets excited about what the teacher is teaching her.

It is *not* okay if our children have no room to feel good about themselves during these years. It is *not* okay to compare one child to another one in the family. It is *not* okay to feel jealous or possessive of our children just because they like a friend's mom or dad. If we feel jealous, we need to figure out why, and then stifle ourselves.

It *is* okay if one child excels at math, another excels at drawing and another excels at auto mechanics. It *is* okay if our children feel good about themselves, even though they haven't gotten straight As or a B-average or whatever our criteria for success happens to be. We know many wealthy, successful people who never finished high school or college. We know many happy, successful, "nonwealthy" people, too. Some of them have high-school diplomas, some have college diplomas and some have Ph.D.'s.

The basic skills that are learned during this stage are how to work, how to get along with other people, how to be social and political people, how to get what we need out of life without alienating everyone around us, and how to feel good about what we do. The specifics of how we do that are not nearly as important as doing it somehow. In rigid families, there is only one right way to do it. In healthier families, there are literally hundreds of ways to do it.

Identity vs. Identity Confusion: Roughly Thirteen to Thirty-Two Years

As we said earlier, the above four stages bring us to the first *adult* stage of our development, which is called *Identity vs. Identity Confusion* (also called Identity Diffusion) somewhere between the ages of eighteen and thirty-two, depending upon how much formal education we get, economic factors and family system factors. Erikson and researchers who have studied his theories believe that there are two key elements in achieving a clear identity:

> 1. Searching
> 2. Commitment

Erikson felt that it was not possible to be a healthy adult with a clear sense of self without going through a *psychosocial moratorium,* which is just a fancy way to say a period of questioning, searching and even some rebellion. We must question our religious beliefs, the values with which we were raised, career choices that our parents may have overtly or covertly made for us, lifestyle preferences and the like. We may come back to those childhood beliefs after this period of questioning, but we will no longer be children when we do, and we won't be doing it "just because someone told us it was the right way to live or think." And we may *not* come back to our childhood beliefs, choosing rather to think and act in some other ways than the ones that were given to us by our parents. One fact remains: If we don't go through this period of searching, we won't get through the identity stage. It is this fact that causes problems for some families.

The *commitment* part of identity formation means that we must eventually make clear choices about our beliefs and lifestyles, and that our choices be more than just verbal ones. We must act on them. A person who chooses monogamy but has extramarital affairs all the time is not committed to monogamy as a lifestyle. A person who claims to be a Christian but who treats his family and employees cruelly is not living his beliefs—he is only talking about them. Children whose parents say one thing but do another struggle greatly with their own integrity.

Based on the depth of the searching we have done, and the strength of our commitment, Erikson delineated four possible identity types, or outcomes of this stage. These four types are:

> 1. Identity Achieved
> 2. Moratorium
> 3. Foreclosed
> 4. Identity Confused (Diffused)

1. Identity Achieved

To get here, we will have struggled with and searched through initial questions of work, religion, sexuality, political beliefs and lifestyle. These may change as we mature, but this is the first time we've been able to do it on a large scale. We have also made clear commitments to our current choices, so that our feelings, beliefs and actions are pretty congruent—that is, they match. Do we have to have a clear commitment to all parts of our choices and ourselves? No, but the fewer commitments we have, the less likely it is that we are identity achieved.

2. Moratorium

We are in the searching period. We are actively struggling. We are trying on different hats. We are dating different people. We are trying out different careers or college majors. But there is something systematic and directed about our search. We have not made clear commitments yet.

3. Foreclosed

There is a good amount of research and theorizing suggesting that close to 50 percent of us are in this state. Foreclosure means that we seem to have a clear set of commitments but we never really went through a search to get there. We go into adulthood wearing the same childhood hats that we've always worn, but the hat is on an adult body. We wear adult suits and ties and dresses and we say adult words, do adult things and tell ourselves that we believe adult beliefs—but deep inside we sense that we still have some things to face.

Growing up is scary. It is sometimes lonely. It means saying good-bye to childhood and making peace with whatever childhood fantasies, as well as demons, that we may have grown up with. Getting out of foreclosure is like standing on the edge of a cliff on a pitch-black, moonless night, and then jumping off without knowing whether the cliff is three feet high or one hundred feet high. Having those four earlier stages filled in fairly well, and having a supportive family behind you, makes this a lot easier.

Moving into adulthood is especially risky for some people because they get an unusual amount of flack when they try. A woman who struggled to end an abusive relationship was told, "You're crazy. That's all there is to it. Any woman would just die to be married to him!" She thought, *I am dying.*

A woman we know was struggling to differentiate. She realized that she was spending up to six hours a day talking to her friends on the phone "about their mutual problems." She said she felt trapped by her need to meet everyone's needs. She struggled for quite some time with the dilemma of hurting others versus hurting herself, and then she decided to take the life-changing step into adulthood by changing the message on her answering machine. When people called, they heard this: "Hi! I really want to talk to you, but I'm swamped! Please leave a message, and I'll get back to you in a couple of days!" We listened to the message and agreed that its tone was kind, honest, caring and yet clear. We said that some people might be angered by it and wondered if she could handle that. A few weeks later, she returned and reported that some people were, indeed, angered by it. She worried about that, but felt proud, too. Several friends called her back and said, "I *love* your message! That's so courageous! I'm thinking of doing the same thing! Thanks!" Cementing an identity happens this way. It isn't about bells and whistles. It's about small changes.

"How could you dare to go back to college? What about me and the kids? Who will be there to do the cooking and the laundry? Who will be there with me every night?" Leaving foreclosure behind is a struggle because it means change, and change is uncomfortable for everyone. By definition, it is a time of turmoil. Some counselors actually label people as "dysfunctional" or "neurotic" when they are simply entering a healthy moratorium in their lives. They are taking the grand risk of becoming adults.

4. Identity Confused (Diffused)

When someone is in this state, he is searching, but it is different from when he is in the moratorium phase. The searching goes in circles. There is no direction to it. He jumps from one lover to the next, from one job or career to the next, from one set of beliefs to the next, and from one lifestyle to the next. He is a lost soul, wandering the Earth looking for a sense of security in a way that he never got when he was growing up. Sometimes he is an offender or an addict who hurts people in the process of wandering.

In college, this person may have been the party king (or the party queen), but he never quite got out of that state.

Or he is the rigid, religious fundamentalist whose identity is defined and controlled by something outside of himself. While he may speak of being an easygoing free spirit, he is far from that. He cannot tolerate differences of opinion because any other opinion would threaten his very sense of self, and that is not tolerable. When a person is identity achieved, a good chunk of his sense of self is comfortably inside of him and cannot be threatened by someone else's point of view.

People ask us how so many people could follow Jim Jones to Guyana and then commit mass suicide with him at his command. We believe that they were identity confused, and that they needed Jim Jones so much for their own self-definition that they were willing to give up the very essence of their self-definition—their own lives.

Getting beyond identity foreclosure or identity confusion requires that we have strong, healthy building blocks when we reach adolescence. It also requires that we look at our childhoods, reevaluate both the "good" and the "bad," and realize that our parents are neither saints nor ogres—they are human beings.

APPENDIX B

The Magic Number 7 Plus or Minus Two

Every once in awhile someone comes along and has such a comprehensive impact on your life that you don't see it for a long, long time. When I was a sophomore in college, wondering what I was supposed to be doing with my life and feeling the need to declare a major, I found myself gravitating toward law more than anything else because I admired my father and the remarkable integrity he displayed in his law career. That preliminary plan served its purpose—to give me *something* to say when people asked what I was going to do with my life. But towards the end of that year, I found myself being grabbed and pulled headlong into psychology by the excellence of two of my professors. One was a clinician who knew how to truly connect with college students, and the other was an experimental psychologist whose enthusiastic, playful love of research and experimentation was infectious to many of his students, including me. I declared a psychology major that spring.

By the time my final year rolled around, we were required to do a senior research experiment in psychology, and I knew exactly what I wanted to do. This energetic professor had somehow managed to get many of us excited by the brand-new field of information processing, in which concepts from the infant field of computer science were being used to help us understand human thinking and memory. In 1956, George A. Miller wrote one of the most famous journal articles in the history of psychology for the prestigious *Psychological Review.* The title of the article was "The Magic Number 7, Plus or Minus Two: Some Limits on Our Capacity for Processing Information."

The "magic number 7" refers to the channel capacity, or the amount of information that a human being can process simultaneously. The key word here is "simultaneously." It can also be described as the number of chunks of information that we can keep in short-term memory at one given moment. For example, if you tell someone a phone number, and they don't have a pen and paper to write it down, most people are able to remember seven numbers. One of the subtests on the Wechsler Adult Intelligence Scale-Revised is called Digit Span. The test administrator reads increasingly long lists of digits, and your task is to repeat them back right away. The average number that people can repeat correctly is "7, plus or minus two."

If you use a mnemonic device, such as rehearsing the list immediately or visualizing the numbers in "chunks" of two or three, then you can usually remember more. The effects of this "chunking" can be seen with telephone numbers. If you already know your area code, you don't have to memorize that when the number is given to you by the operator, because "651" or "520" is now *one* number to you. If you know your area code and seven-digit phone number, then adding a four-digit password for a calling card is a piece of cake. All you really have to remember is "my entire phone number" plus "3791." The magic number is "7 plus or minus two" because the range for most human beings is from five to nine. That's what I did my senior research project on, and it was the beginning of a lifelong love of the scientific side of psychology. Most of the clinical side came later.

The number "seven" is one of those biblical numbers. It appears with significance in almost every culture. And there it was, popping up as one of the most significant pieces of research and experimental thought of the mid- to late-1900s. When it comes to complex stimuli like people's faces, complex tastes or smells, or complex emotions, human beings can remember many more than seven. But if you think about it, when it comes to lists, seven is about the limit of what people are willing or able to handle. A list of seven, like seven shades of gray, seven different sizes of circles or squares, or seven gradations on a rating scale (from "1-Never" to "7-Always") is able to keep our attention, because we are able to keep its seven elements in mind all at one time. In other words, a list of seven often allows the reader to form a single, coherent mental picture.

And so we have 7. That magic number. And thanks to Lawrence E. Murphy, Ph.D., for being the first of many to delight my mind with the wonders of psychology.

John C. Friel, Ph.D.

ENDNOTES

1. John M. Gottman, *Why Marriages Succeed or Fail* (New York: Simon and Schuster, 1994).
2. Y. Shoda, W. Mischel, and P. K. Peake, "Predicting Adolescent Cognitive and Self-Regulatory Competencies from Preschool Delay of Gratification," *Developmental Psychology* 26 (1990): 978–86.
3. Gottman, 1.
4. Salvador Minuchin, *Families and Family Therapy* (Cambridge: Harvard University Press, 1974).
5. Elisabeth Kübler-Ross, *On Death and Dying* (New York: Macmillan, 1969).
6. John M. Gottman and Nan Silver, *The Seven Principles for Making Marriage Work* (New York: Crown Publishers, 1999).
7. Peter Koestenbaum, *Existential Sexuality: Choosing to Love* (Englewood Cliffs, N.J.: Prentice-Hall, 1974), 20.
8. Salvador Minuchin, "Couple/Family Therapy," The Milton H. Erickson Foundation Evolution of Psychotherapy Conference, Anaheim, California, May 25–29, 2000.

9. Jay Lebow, "What 'Really' Makes Couples Happy? A Controversy Divides the World of Marital Researchers," *Family Therapy Networker* (Jan./Feb. 2001): 59–62.

10. Catherine Johnson, *Lucky in Love: The Secrets of Happy Couples and How Their Marriages Thrive* (New York: Viking, 1992).

11. Abraham H. Maslow, "The Authoritarian Character Structure," *Journal of Social Psychology* 18 (1943): 401–11.

12. John Steinbeck, *Cannery Row* (New York: Viking, 1945), 1.

13. Harville Hendrix, *Getting the Love You Want: A Guide for Couples* (New York: Henry Holt, 1988).

14. Kübler-Ross, 6.

15. Erik H. Erikson, *Identity: Youth and Crisis* (New York: W. W. Norton and Co., Inc., 1986).

16. Murray Bowen, *Family Therapy in Clinical Practice* (New York: Jason Aronson, 1978).

17. Jacob L. Orlofsky, James E. Marcia, and Ira M. Lesser, "Ego Identity Status and the Intimacy Versus Isolation Crisis of Young Adulthood," *Journal of Personality and Social Psychology* 27 (1973): 211–19.

18. Martin Buber, *I and Thou* (New York: Scribner, 1974).

19. David M. Schnarch, *Passionate Marriage: Sex, Love and Intimacy in Emotionally Committed Relationships* (New York: W. W. Norton, 1997), 259.

20. James W. Maddock and Noel R. Larson, *Incestuous Families: An Ecological Approach to Understanding and Treatment* (New York: W. W. Norton, 1995), 51.

21. Peter Koestenbaum, *Existential Sexuality: Choosing to Love* (Englewood Cliffs, N.J.: Prentice-Hall, 1974).

22. Patricia Love and Jo Robinson, *Hot Monogamy: Essential Steps to More Passionate Lovemaking* (New York: Penguin, 1995), 260.

23. Quotez Web site *www.geocities.com/Athens/Oracle/6517/sex.htm*.

24. Paul Reiser, *Couplehood* (New York: Bantam Books, 1995), 274.

25. Johnson, 152.

26. See also David M. Schnarch, *Constructing the Sexual Crucible: An Integration of Sexual and Marital Therapy* (New York: W. W. Norton, 1991).

27. The connection between differentiation and healthy sexuality has also been emphasized by L. C. Wynne and A. R. Wynne, "The Quest for Intimacy," *Journal of Marital and Family Therapy* 12 (1986): 383–94.

28. John C. Friel, *Rescuing Your Spirit: When Third-Grade Morality Isn't Enough for Christians* (Deerfield Beach, Fla.: Health Communications, Inc., 1993).

29. Ibid. References for this quote are as follows: "Sex and Religion: Churches, the Bible and Furor over Modern Sexuality," *U.S. News & World Report,* 10 June 1991. James B. Nelson, *Embodiment* (Minneapolis: Augsburg Publishing House, 1978).

30. John MacMurray, *Reason and Emotion* (London: Faber and Faber, 1935), 39.

31. Mary Matalin and James Carville, with Peter Knobler, *All's Fair: Love, War and Running for President* (New York: Random House, 1994), 469–70.

32. Harriet Lerner, *The Dance of Intimacy: A Woman's Guide to Courageous Acts of Change in Key Relationships* (San Francisco: HarperCollins, 1990).

33. For example, see the following: Susan S. Hendrick and Clyde Hendrick, *Liking, Loving and Relating* (Pacific Grove, Calif.: Brooks/Cole Publishing, 1992); or, Doug Jones, *Physical Attractiveness and the Theory of Sexual Selection: Results from Five Populations* (Ann Arbor, Mich.: Museum of Anthropology Publications, 1996).

34. There are numerous birth-order theories. The information we present here is a mix of the work of the late Minneapolis psychiatrist Jerry Bach, as well as the well-known work of Alfred Adler.

35. The title of the film is *Remember Me.*

36. Ann Petrie and Jeanette Petrie, *Mother Teresa* (Petrie Productions, 1985).

37. Karl Rahner, *The Spirit in the Church* (New York: Seabury Press, 1979), 12.

38. The history cited here is from Richard E. Friel, personal communication, and the Boston University Web site entitled the *Dictionary of Modern Western Theology (www.bu.edu/wwildman/WeirdWildWeb/index.htm),* articles by Phil LaFountain and JeeHo Kim. Cited in the articles was J. Peter Schineller, "Discovering Jesus Christ: A History We Share," in *A World of Grace: An Introduction to the Themes and Foundations of Karl Rahner's Theology,* ed. Leo J. O'Donovan (New York: The Crossroad Publishing Company, 1991).

39. Donna Halvorsen, "Judge Faults Arrest, Drops Charges in High-Profile Drunken-Driving Case," *Minneapolis StarTribune,* 20 Apr. 1995: B1.

40. Miles Corwin, "Mother Turns Grief, Grit to Memorial for Slain Son," *Los Angeles Times,* 29 Oct. 1995: A27–A28.

41. Daniel Goleman, *Emotional Intelligence: Why It Can Matter More Than IQ* (New York: Bantam, 1995).

42. Gottman, *Why Marriages Succeed or Fail.*

43. Redford Williams and Virginia Williams, *Anger Kills: Seventeen Strategies for Controlling the Hostility That Can Harm Your Health* (New York: HarperPerennial, 1994).

44. Gershen Kaufman, *Shame, the Power of Caring* (Cambridge, Mass.: Schenkman Publishing Company, 1980).

45. Dean Ornish, *Love and Survival: The Scientific Basis for the Healing Power of Intimacy* (New York: HarperCollins, 1998).

46. James Masterson, *The Search for the Real Self: Unmasking the Personality Disorders of Our Age* (New York: The Free Press, 1988).

47. Martin E. P. Seligman, *Learned Optimism: How to Change Your Mind and Your Life* (New York: Alfred A. Knopf, 1991).

48. Ornish, 39.

49. Personal communication, 2000.

50. Schnarch, *Passionate Marriage: Sex, Love and Intimacy in Emotionally Committed Relationships,* 56.

51. John C. Friel and Linda D. Friel, *Adult Children: The Secrets of Dysfunctional Families* (Deerfield Beach, Fla.: Health Communications, Inc., 1988), 133.

52. Personal communication, 1995.

53. Jean Piaget, *The Origin of Intelligence in Children* (New York: International Universities Press, 1936).

54. James W. Maddock and Noel R. Larson, *Incestuous Families: An Ecological Approach to Understanding and Treatment* (New York: W. W. Norton, 1995).

55. Ibid.

56. William J. Doherty, *Take Back Your Marriage: Sticking Together in a World That Pulls Us Apart* (New York: Guilford Press, 2001).

57. August Wilson, *Two Trains Running* (New York: Penguin Books, 1993).

58. Stephen Gilligan, "Getting to the Core," *Family Therapy Networker* (Jan./Feb. 2001): 24.

59. Adam Gopnik, "Man Goes to See a Doctor," *The New Yorker,* 24 and 31 Aug. 1998: 114–21.

60. Ibid, p. 121.

61. Wilhelm Stekel, quoted in *Time,* 18 June 2001: 66.

62. William Shakespeare, *Macbeth,* c. 1605.

63. These facts and quotes about authors are from *www.rejectionslips.com/wisdom.html.*

64. Jane Ammeson, "Maya Angelou Uncaged," *Northwest Airlines WorldTraveler,* May 2001: 43.

65. "The soft white lei encircles the crest of the mountain, the mountain high above, standing in great majesty, majestic on high, veiled in clouds." Description of Mauna Kea, The White Mountain, by Nona Beamer,

from the liner to the CD *Mauna Kea: White Mountain Journal,* by Keola Beamer, Dancing Cat Records, Windham Hill Records, BMG Distribution, New York, 1997.

66. Ibid.

67. Adapted from John C. Friel and Linda D. Friel, *Adult Children: The Secrets of Dysfunctional Families* (Deerfield Beach, Fla.: Health Communications, Inc., 1988).

REFERENCES

Ammeson, Jane. "Maya Angelou Uncaged." *Northwest Airlines WorldTraveler,* May 2001.

Bowen, Murray. *Family Therapy in Clinical Practice.* New York: Jason Aronson, 1978.

Bradbury, Ray. *Fahrenheit 451: 40th Anniversary Edition.* New York: Simon & Schuster, 1993.

————. Invited address for the Pen Pals Lecture Series, Library Foundation of Hennepin County, Minnesota. Spring 2000.

Buber, Martin. *I and Thou.* New York: Scribner, 1974.

Cheever, John. *The Stories of John Cheever.* New York: Alfred A. Knopf, 1978.

Corwin, Miles. "Mother Turns Grief, Grit to Memorial for Slain Son." *Los Angeles Times,* 29 October 1995: A27–A28.

Doherty, William J. *Take Back Your Marriage: Sticking Together in a World That Pulls Us Apart.* New York: Guilford Press, 2001.

Erikson, Erik H. *Identity: Youth and Crisis.* New York: W. W. Norton and Co., Inc., 1986.

Fields, Rick, Peggy Taylor, and R. Weyler. *Chop Wood, Carry Water: A Guide to Finding Spiritual Fulfillment in Everyday Life.* New York: Jeremy Tarcher, 1985.

Friel, Brian. *Selected Plays.* London: Faber and Faber, 1984.

Friel, John C. *Rescuing Your Spirit: When Third-Grade Morality Isn't Enough for Christians.* Deerfield Beach, Fla.: Health Communications, Inc., 1993.

Friel, John C., and Linda D. Friel. *Adult Children: The Secrets of Dysfunctional Families.* Deerfield Beach, Fla.: Health Communications, Inc., 1988.

Gilligan, Stephen. "Getting to the Core." *Family Therapy Networker,* January/February, 2001: 22 ff.

Goleman, D. *Emotional Intelligence: Why It Can Matter More Than IQ.* New York: Bantam, 1995.

Gopnik, Adam. "Man Goes to See a Doctor." *The New Yorker,* 24 and 31 August 1998: 114–21.

Gottman, John M. *Why Marriages Succeed or Fail.* New York: Simon and Schuster, 1994.

Gottman, John M., and Nan Silver. *The Seven Principles for Making Marriage Work.* New York: Crown Publishers, 1999.

Guterson, David. *Snow Falling on Cedars.* New York: Vintage Books, 1995.

Halvorsen, Donna. "Judge Faults Arrest, Drops Charges in

High-Profile Drunken-Driving Case." *Minneapolis StarTribune,* 20 April 1995: B1.

Hawking, Stephen W. *A Brief History of Time: From the Big Bang to Black Holes.* New York: Bantam Books, 1988.

Hendrick, Susan S., and Clyde Hendrick. *Liking, Loving and Relating.* Pacific Grove, Calif: Brooks/Cole Publishing, 1992.

Hendrix, Harville. *Getting the Love You Want: A Guide for Couples.* New York: Henry Holt, 1988.

Hoeg, Peter. *Miss Smilla's Feeling for Snow.* London: HarperCollins Publishers, 1994.

Huxley, Aldous. *Two or Three Graces.* Quoted in Dunaway, David King. *Huxley in Hollywood.* New York: Harper & Row, 1989.

Johnson, Catherine. *Lucky in Love: The Secrets of Happy Couples and How Their Marriages Thrive.* New York: Viking, 1992.

Jones, Doug. *Physical Attractiveness and the Theory of Sexual Selection: Results from Five Populations.* Ann Arbor, Mich.: Museum of Anthropology Publications, 1996.

Kaufman, G. *Shame, the Power of Caring.* Cambridge, Mass.: Schenkman Publishing Company, 1980.

Koestenbaum, Peter. *Existential Sexuality: Choosing to Love.* Englewood Cliffs, N.J.: Prentice-Hall, 1974.

Kübler-Ross, Elisabeth. *On Death and Dying.* New York: Macmillan, 1969.

Lebow, Jay. "What 'Really' Makes Couples Happy? A Controversy Divides the World of Marital Researchers." *Family Therapy Networker,* January/February 2001: 59–62.

Lerner, Harriet. *The Dance of Intimacy: A Woman's Guide to Courageous Acts of Change in Key Relationships.* San Francisco: HarperCollins, 1990.

Lethem, Jonathan. *Motherless Brooklyn.* New York: Vintage Books, 1999.

Lopez, Barry. *About This Life: Journeys on the Threshold of Memory.* New York: Alfred A. Knopf, 1998.

Love, Patricia, and Jo Robinson. *Hot Monogamy: Essential Steps to More Passionate Lovemaking.* New York: Penguin, 1995.

MacMurray, John. *Reason and Emotion.* London: Faber and Faber, 1935.

Maddock, James W., and Noel R. Larson. *Incestuous Families: An Ecological Approach to Understanding and Treatment.* New York: W.W. Norton, 1995.

Marquez, Gabriel Garcia. *Love in the Time of Cholera.* New York: Penguin Books, 1989.

Maslow, Abraham H. "The Authoritarian Character Structure." *Journal of Social Psychology* 18 (1943): 401–11.

Masterson, James. *The Search for the Real Self: Unmasking the Personality Disorders of Our Age.* New York: The Free Press, 1988.

Matalin, Mary, and James Carville, with Peter Knobler. *All's Fair: Love, War and Running for President.* New York: Random House, 1994.

Minuchin, Salvador. *Families and Family Therapy.* Cambridge: Harvard University Press, 1974.

———. "Couple/Family Therapy." Address to The Milton H. Erickson Foundation Evolution of Psychotherapy Conference, Anaheim, Calif., May 25–29, 2000.

Orlofsky, Jacob L., James E. Marcia, & Ira M. Lesser. "Ego Identity Status and the Intimacy Versus Isolation Crisis of Young Adulthood." *Journal of Personality and Social Psychology* 27 (1973): 211–19.

Ornish, Dean. *Love and Survival: The Scientific Basis for the Healing Power of Intimacy.* New York: HarperCollins, 1998.

Petrie, A., and J. Petrie. *Mother Teresa.* Petrie Productions, 1985.

Piaget, J. *The Origin of Intelligence in Children.* New York: International Universities Press, 1936.

Pirsig, Robert. *Zen and the Art of Motorcycle Maintenance: An Inquiry into Values.* New York: William Morrow & Company, Inc., 1974.

Rahner, Karl. *The Spirit in the Church.* New York: Seabury Press, 1979.

Reiser, Paul. *Couplehood.* New York: Bantam Books, 1995.

Schleiermacher, Friedrich. *On Religion: Speeches to Its*

Cultured Despisers. Cambridge, Mass.: Cambridge University Press, 1988.

Schnarch, David M. *Constructing the Sexual Crucible: An Integration of Sexual and Marital Therapy.* New York: W. W. Norton, 1991.

————. *Passionate Marriage: Sex, Love and Intimacy in Emotionally Committed Relationships.* New York: W. W. Norton, 1997.

Seligman, Martin E. P. *Learned Optimism: How to Change Your Mind and Your Life.* New York: Alfred A. Knopf, 1991.

Shoda, Y., W. Mischel, and P. K. Peake. "Predicting Adolescent Cognitive and Self-Regulatory Competencies from Preschool Delay of Gratification." *Developmental Psychology* 26 (1990): 978–86.

Steinbeck, John. *Cannery Row.* New York: Viking, 1945.

Stekel, Wilhelm. *Time,* 18 June 2001: 66.

Stoppard, Tom. *Arcadia.* London: Faber and Faber, 1993.

Theroux, Peter. *Translating L.A.: A Tour of the Rainbow City.* New York: W. W. Norton, 1994.

Upton, Charles. *Hammering Hot Iron: A Spiritual Critique of Bly's Iron John.* Wheaton, Ill.: Quest Books, 1993.

Williams, Redford, and Virginia Williams. *Anger Kills: Seventeen Strategies for Controlling the Hostility That Can Harm Your Health.* New York: HarperPerennial, 1994.

Wilson, August. *Two Trains Running.* New York: Penguin Books, 1993.

INDEX

313

ABOUT THE AUTHORS

John C. Friel, Ph.D., and Linda D. Friel, M.A., are licensed psychologists in private practice in New Brighton, a suburb of Minneapolis/St. Paul. John is also licensed in Nevada. They have three grown children who have left the nest, as well as a female Labrador retriever and a male cockapoo who live at home with them. The Friels do individual, couple and family therapy, ongoing men's and women's therapy groups, as well as seminars and workshops in the United States, Canada, England and Ireland, for the general public, hospitals, corporations, universities and government agencies. They also conduct the ClearLife/ Lifeworks Clinic in several U.S. locations. The clinic is a gentle three-and-a-half-day process designed to help participants discover old patterns that are tripping them up in the present, and to begin to create new patterns that are healthier.

ClearLife for Couples™ is the program they designed to help people in long-term relationships identify *their own part* in how they can create a really great relationship. It is structured along similar lines as the original ClearLife/ Lifeworks Clinic.

They are the bestselling authors of *Adult Children: The Secrets of Dysfunctional Families; An Adult Child's Guide to What's "Normal"; The Grown-Up Man: Heroes, Healing, Honor, Hurt, Hope; Rescuing Your Spirit; The Soul of Adulthood: Opening the Doors; The 7 Worst Things (Good) Parents Do; The 7 Best Things (Smart) Teens Do;* and *The 7 Best Things (Happy) Couples Do.*

The Friels have been featured on or in ABC News' *20/20,* the *Oprah Winfrey Show,* MSNBC, *USA Today, Parents* magazine, *Pregnancy* magazine, *Redbook, Child* magazine, *The Dr. Toni Grant Show* and scores of other radio and television programs and newspapers across the country.

They can be contacted at:

Friel Associates/ClearLife/Lifeworks
P.O. Box 120148
New Brighton, MN 55112
phone: 651-628-0220
fax: 651-628-4909
Web site: *www.clearlife.com*

Their Web site, which includes books, tapes, speaking schedules and a monthly psychology (mostly) column written by their two dogs, *Minnesota Sam & Abby,* is located at *www.clearlife.com,* or you can go to *www.johnfriel.com* or *www.lindafriel.com.*

John's parent-training video, *How to Talk to Children About Difficult Things,* is due for release soon. Please check their Web site for further details.

More From
John and Linda Friel

New York Times BESTSELLER

THE 7 WORST THINGS (good) PARENTS DO

John C. Friel, Ph.D.
Linda D. Friel, M.A.

Code 6684 • Paperback • $10.95

You may not like everything you read in this life-changing book, but once you implement the Friels' suggestions, you'll love this book—and the difference in your children's behavior.

This book was written expressly for teens as a unique road map from the teen years to adulthood. It was designed to stimulate the brain as well as the heart, because teenagers who listen to both eventually negotiate adolescence successfully.

THE 7 BEST THINGS (smart) TEENS DO

John C. Friel, Ph.D.
Linda D. Friel, M.A.

Code 777X • Paperback • $12.95

Also From *New York Times* Best-Selling Authors John and Linda Friel